The DESERT ISLANDS *of* ~~MEXICO'S~~ SEA *of* CORTEZ

◀ STEWART AITCHISON ▶

The DESERT ISLANDS *of* MEXICO'S SEA *of* CORTEZ

The University of Arizona Press
Tucson

The University of Arizona Press
www.uapress.arizona.edu

Printed in the United States of America

ISBN-13: 978-0-8165-2774-8

Cover designed by Barbara Haines
Cover photo by the author

Library of Congress Cataloging-in-Publication Data
Aitchison, Stewart W.
The desert islands of Mexico's Sea of Cortez / Stewart Aitchison.
p. cm.
Includes bibliographical references.
ISBN 978-0-8165-2774-8 (pbk. : alk. paper)
1. Natural history—Mexico—California, Gulf of, Region. 2. Environmental
degradation—Mexico—California, Gulf of, Region. 3. California, Gulf of, Region
(Mexico)—Environmental conditions. 4. Desert ecology—Mexico—California,
Gulf of, Region. 5. Island ecology—Mexico—California, Gulf of, Region. 6. Baja
California Region (Mexico : Peninsula)—Environmental conditions. I. Title.
QH107.A523 2010
508.72'2—dc22

2010006135

♾ This paper meets the requirements of ANSI/NISO Z39.48-1992
(Permanence of Paper).

▲

To Peter Butz, Pamela Fingleton, Sven-Olof Lindblad, Marie Ciccone, and the other great Lindblad Expeditions folks who were instrumental in leading me down this wonderful, serendipitous course of my life.

▼

Contents

Illustrations

Acknowledgments

For more than a quarter of a century, I have had the privilege to visit and explore the desert islands of the Sea of Cortez with Lindblad Expeditions, accompanied by a cadre of scientists, naturalists, photographers, artists, and intrepid tourists. These individuals include Linda Burback, Karen Copeland, Dennis Cornejo, Alberto Montaudon Ferrer, Bryan Gates, Lindy Birkel Hopkins, Ian McTaggert-Cowan, Pete Pederson, Gretchen Pederson, Pete Puleston, Berit Solstad, Rikki Swenson, and Enriqueta Velarde. Others, who are now gone but not forgotten, include George Lindsay, Ken Norris, Dennis Puleston, and Ted Walker. Special thanks to Richard Brusca, William Lopez Forment, Ralph Lee Hopkins, Jim Kelley, Carlos Navarro-Serment, Wayne Ranney, Jack Swenson, and Tom Whitham for reviewing sections of the manuscript and providing corrections and helpful suggestions. Freelance copyeditor Sharon E. Hunt did a remarkable job of improving my grammar and clearing up my ambiguities. Any remaining errors are mine alone. The good people at the University of Arizona Press, especially Patti Hartmann, senior acquiring editor; Nancy Arora, production editor; Barbara Yarrow, editing and production manager; and Arin Cumming, exhibits manager, get the credit for putting all the pieces together. Thanks to all of you.

The DESERT ISLANDS *of* MEXICO'S SEA *of* CORTEZ

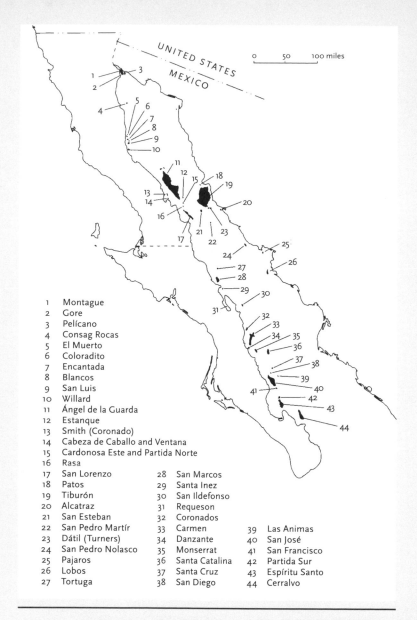

1   Montague
2   Gore
3   Pelícano
4   Consag Rocas
5   El Muerto
6   Coloradito
7   Encantada
8   Blancos
9   San Luis
10   Willard
11   Ángel de la Guarda
12   Estanque
13   Smith (Coronado)
14   Cabeza de Caballo and Ventana
15   Cardonosa Este and Partida Norte
16   Rasa

17	San Lorenzo		
18	Patos		
19	Tiburón		
20	Alcatraz		
21	San Esteban		
22	San Pedro Martír		
23	Dátil (Turners)		
24	San Pedro Nolasco		
25	Pajaros		
26	Lobos		
27	Tortuga	28	San Marcos
		29	Santa Inez
		30	San Ildefonso
		31	Requeson
		32	Coronados
		33	Carmen
		34	Danzante	39	Las Animas
		35	Monserrat	40	San José
		36	Santa Catalina	41	San Francisco
		37	Santa Cruz	42	Partida Sur
		38	San Diego	43	Espíritu Santo
				44	Cerralvo

FIGURE 1   The Mexican Comisión Nacional de Áreas Naturales Protegidas counts 922 islands and islets in the Sea of Cortez. This map shows 44 of the larger islands.

Introduction

The Sea of Cortez—it's a romantic name that conjures up visions of fiery sunsets, leaping dolphins, and deserted beaches. Between the Baja Peninsula and mainland Mexico, the roughly 800-mile-long, on average 95-mile-wide, sparkling Gulf of California is dotted with a myriad of dramatic, stony, desert islands that at first blush may appear lifeless and foreboding. But the intrepid explorer is surprised to discover in that stark landscape a host of plants and animals well suited to the arid, unforgiving, sun-bleached environment. Some have called the islands "the Mexican Galápagos," and famous ocean explorer and scientist Jacques-Yves Cousteau referred to the surrounding bountiful sea as "the aquarium of the world." In 2005, UNESCO recognized much of the gulf and its islands as a World Heritage Site.

Although I grew up only a half-day's drive from the Sea of Cortez, I was ignorant about its remarkable islands and rich waters until I began to work for Lindblad Expeditions aboard a small ship providing natural history cruises around the Baja Peninsula. In 1981, I was hired to be a naturalist—not because I knew a lick about whales or sea birds, but because I was versed in Sonoran Desert biology and lore. As the days have passed into weeks and the weeks have passed into dozens of seasons, I have had the good fortune to travel and work with many leading experts in the natural and human history of this extraordinary area. I hope that I have retained some of their scholarship.

However, I don't want to leave you with the impression that all of the secrets of the Sea of Cortez and its islands have been uncovered

FIGURE 2 Exploring the islands in a small boat.

and revealed to me—they certainly have not. But there is a foundation of knowledge, which is being added to each year. This slim volume
recounts some of what is known and a little of what is suspected, asks a
few pertinent and impertinent questions, and speculates on the future
of this special sea and its unique desert islands.

The gulf can be divided into three major regions. The upper region's
basin is astoundingly deep—up to three miles in depth when measured
to bedrock—but it is almost entirely filled in with sand and silt depos-
ited by the Colorado River's delta over millions of years. Today, the sea
depth in the upper gulf is no more than six hundred feet. This area experiences the greatest seasonal temperature fluctuations and the least
amount of rain, and its waters are highly saline. Only a handful of small
islands are found here.

It's also a region of extreme tides of more than thirty vertical feet. The
extraordinary tidal changes in the upper gulf can surprise the unwary.
The first time I took a kayak out in the sea there, I was so anxious to
get on the water that I didn't think about tides. My wife Ann, our baby
daughter Kate, and I climbed into the double kayak and shoved off,

apparently during high tide. Off we paddled, enjoying a lovely day on an ocean as flat as a mirror. Overhead, prehistoric-looking brown pelicans streamed by in long lines and startled fish jumped out of the sea. We paddled some, bobbed around like a cork a little, ate some snacks, and sipped cold drinks.

Finally, it was time to head back to shore. We could see our car parked on the beach maybe several hundred yards away. We dug in with our paddles, went a few strokes, and suddenly ran aground. The water was only a few inches deep. Where had the ocean gone? Oh yeah, it's low tide.

Now we had a dilemma. We could wait for the tide to turn, or we could drag our craft across the mud flat. We chose to do the latter. I picked up our daughter and carried her and a camera case about fifty yards. I put the case down on the exposed gooey ocean bottom, sat Kate on top of it, and told her to wait as Mom and Dad dragged the kayak to her. Then we repeated the process several times. Slowly, we made it back to the dry beach. Now when I am near the sea, I think about tides—a lot.

Traveling south, you come to the Midriff Islands area, which contains roughly a dozen major islands, including the gulf's two largest—Islas Ángel de la Guarda and Tiburón—which are separated from each other and the peninsula by trenches up to a mile deep. Maximum tides of around fourteen feet are accompanied by strong tidal currents, which have frustrated sailors for centuries. In the early 1700s, Jesuit Father Juan de Ugarte tried to sail his sloop northward between Isla San Lorenzo and the peninsula, but gave up after twenty days of fighting the currents and wind. That particular channel appropriately became known as Canal de Salsipuedes—"get out if you can."

The southern gulf region extends roughly from Santa Rosalía southward to the tip of the Baja Peninsula and contains the remaining twenty or so major islands. In this area, the sea gets progressively deeper, with some of the basins reaching more than twelve thousand feet in depth, possibly deeper to bedrock. Tidal variation is much less evident here than in the gulf's upper region, although there is more mixing of these waters with the open Pacific Ocean.

Besides the forty-four major islands shown on the map in figure 1, there are more than nine hundred smaller islands and emerging rocks scattered about. There are also plenty of barely submerged boulders and pinnacles, which at times have proven hazardous to boats and ships.

George Lindsay, eminent botanist and former director of the California Academy of Science, praised the region as "a desert garden of startling beauty." Biologists consider the islands part of the greater Sonoran Desert, which covers northwest mainland Mexico, most of the Baja Peninsula, and parts of southern Arizona and southeastern California. It defies the popular conception of a desert as a lifeless place by supporting about 3,500 vascular plant species. Of the 695 or so identified species growing on the gulf's islands, more than 120 are cacti. At least twenty genera of vascular plants are endemics; that is, they are species found on only one or a few of the islands. The islands are also among the richest in the world in terms of reptile diversity: at least 50 species are endemics. The islands are an evolutionary treasure, home to the largest number of endemic species of plants and animals in North America.

There are three main environmental factors that combine to make this part of the world a dry place. First, the gulf area falls under a region of the earth where there is often descending dry air. The short explanation has to do with global circulation patterns; most of the world's major deserts occur within these so-called horse latitudes, areas of subsiding dry air and persistent high pressure.

Second, off the west coast of the Baja Peninsula is a cold ocean current that flows north to south. As low-pressure storms are spawned in the Pacific Ocean and move on the prevailing easterly winds, they must pass over this relatively cold water. Water vapor condenses, and fog and rain are squeezed out of the weather disturbance before making landfall.

Third, storms that do manage to make it to the Baja Peninsula are forced upward by orographic uplift. In other words, the mountain spine running down much of the length of the peninsula pushes the moisture to higher and cooler heights, and rain and sometimes snow falls at these higher elevations, leaving the gulf on the leeward side in the rain shadow.

Many biologists define a desert as a place that receives less than ten inches of precipitation per year. The Midriff Islands area complies by rarely getting any more than that and usually getting much less, averaging less than five inches annually, with the northern part of the gulf being more parched. Sonoran Desert summers are scorching hot, and the winters are quite mild, with freezing temperatures rare. The scant moisture tends to come at two different times of the year.

FIGURE 3   The broad Arroyo Limantour allows easy access into the interior of Isla San Esteban, where visitors hope to glimpse giant pinto chuckwallas (*Sauromalus varius*) and spiny-tailed iguanas (*Ctenosaura conspicuosa*).

This latter fact is believed to be a major factor in the greater plant and animal diversity found in the Sonoran Desert compared to North America's three other major deserts—the Great Basin, Chihuahua, and Mojave. Since the moisture is spread out during the year, different plants and animals have evolved to utilize the precipitation at a particular time. About half of the flora is tropical or subtropical in origin and tends to use the summer moisture, whereas the winter rains bring on a flourish of ephemerals. Keep in mind, though, that the rainfall in the gulf area is not always this regimented. In some years, the islands may not receive any rain; whereas in other seasons, they may experience flooding.

Another characteristic that distinguishes the Sonoran Desert from the other North American deserts is that it has two dominant plant types: legume trees (e.g., palo verde, mesquite, catclaw acacia, and ironwood) and columnar cacti (e.g., organ pipe, saguaro, and cardón). The legume trees generally have incredibly long roots that search out water far underground. The legumes enrich the poor desert soil by fixing nitrogen out of the air and transporting some of it to their roots. Nitrogen is also released when their leaves and seed pods fall off and decompose. On the other hand, the cacti have shallow root systems that allow them to soak up any rain seeping into the ground. Their stems swell with the moisture and store it for the drier times ahead.

One bright and warm spring day after a rather wet winter, I took a small group of Lindblad Expeditions guests for a natural history stroll up one of the beckoning arroyos on Isla Santa Catalina. The granitic-derived sand is carpeted blue with desert lupines (*Lupinus* spp.). Green-barked palo verde trees (*Cercidium* spp.) are ablaze with yellow blossoms being worked by busy bees. Juanita (*Cardiospermum corindum*) and the endemic mélon de coyote (*Ibervillea sonorae*) and wild spiny cucumber (*Vaseyanthus insularis*) vines are draped over giant barrel cactus (*Ferocactus diguetii*), pitahaya agria (*Stenocereus gummosus*), and cardón (*Pachycereus pringlei*). But in many years, the ephemerals are absent, the perennials are drab and wrinkled, and only a few tough leathery-leaved plants or those with chlorophyll in their stems are photosynthesizing. Everything else, including leafless brown shrubs, buried seeds, and pulpy underground bulbs, are waiting, patiently waiting, for the next thirst-quenching rain.

Yet desert succulents, such as cacti, have a remarkable way of continuing to photosynthesize even under extremely arid conditions. Generally, plants have small openings on their leaves or stems, called stomates, that are open during the day to exchange gases—carbon dioxide in and oxygen out. However, such a system can also allow water to transpire from the plant. Succulents get around this dilemma by opening their stomates at night, when temperatures are cooler and the relative humidity is higher. Carbon dioxide is absorbed and stored as an organic acid. During the day, the stomates are shut tight. Photosynthesis takes place using the stored carbon dioxide. This process was first discovered in the stonecrop family (Crassulaceae) and is now known as crassulacean acid

FIGURE 4 After a rare wet winter, the normally parched desert island plants can be wrapped in luxuriant green growth and surrounded by colorful annuals such as lupines.

metabolism, or CAM for short. Plants using CAM lose only a tenth as much water as those using standard photosynthesis.

Plants are not the only desert residents of the gulf area. Although claims of humans living along the northern Sonora coast as long ago as thirty thousand to forty thousand years are controversial, it is certain that native peoples have been visiting and sometimes living on the islands for thousands of years. Recorded history of the gulf only begins in 1533 when Spanish conquistador Hernán Cortés dispatched the ship *Concepción* to search for a rumored island called California lying off the Pacific coast of Mexico. Stories of pearls, gold, mermaids, and Amazons circulated, but this expedition was doomed from its inception. Captain Diego Becerra de Mendoza's mean temper and arrogant behavior did not sit well with the crew. After days of sailing without sighting land, the men became anxious about their dreadful situation. The ship's pilot, Fortún Jiménez, murdered the captain in his sleep and took command of the ship.

A short time later, the ship found its way into Bahía de La Paz on the east coast of Baja, where the hapless explorers encountered Guaycura Indians. Although apparently a friendly initial encounter, it wasn't long before the Guaycura came to distrust the sailors. Twenty-three sailors were killed while refilling their water barrels. The remaining crew members escaped and returned to mainland Mexico.

Further exploration of the area remained fraught with danger and difficulties. The sea could suddenly become wild with breaking waves and strong currents. In 1539, Spanish explorer Francisco de Ulloa successfully sailed to the head of the gulf, establishing that Baja California was a peninsula rather than an island, a fact that was soon forgotten. Not until a century and half later in 1706 did Spanish explorer Father Eusebio Kino's overland exploration re-establish that Baja California was not an island.

Although other Spanish explorers did find pearls (which continued to lure adventurers and entrepreneurs into the gulf for centuries) and a few deposits of valuable minerals, it was the sea's abundant fish that drew most European settlers. Unfortunately, most of the native population quickly disappeared due to disease, warfare, and displacement. Lack of freshwater kept most of the islands uninhabited except for temporary, seasonal fishing camps. As recently as 1960, nature writer Joseph Wood Krutch could rejoice that "it [the Baja Peninsula] is a land of delight, one where it is possible to escape for a time into a world still what nature rather than human forces have made it."

However, by 1973, Mexican Highway 1, running the length of the peninsula, was finished, and what had been a grueling, dusty, multi-week journey became a relatively easy five- or six-day drive. Today, more and more visitors are discovering Baja California and also venturing out to the islands. The desert peninsula and islands are under siege. But more about this later. For now, join me by ship, Zodiac, kayak, and on foot to explore these desert islands in the Sea of Cortez.

SEA NAMES

Here is a short history of some of the appellations attached to this body of seawater. Indigenous people no doubt had their own names for this sea, but for the most part those words have vanished along with their creators. Spanish explorer Francisco de Ulloa named it Mar Bermejo (Vermilion Sea) because of the color of the water, when in late winter and early spring about two dozen species of dinoflagellates—tiny marine protists (plankton organisms that are sort of a combination of plant and animal)— "bloom" in such large numbers that they give the water a reddish cast. Another version says that he saw the suspended red mud from the Colorado River.

Not long after de Ulloa's voyage, Spaniards began to use the name Mar de Cortés (Sea of Cortés). However, by the mid-1700s, the French replaced the "s" in Cortés with a "z," and that spelling became U.S. anglicized in the 1800s. Also, sometime in the late 1500s, the name Golfo de California (Gulf of California) began to be popular. I am going to use both Gulf of California and Sea of Cortez for no particular reason other than I like both names. Readers can look up Richard C. Brusca's Introduction in his *The Gulf of California: Biodiversity and Conservation* for more details about the history of the names in this region.

The Big Split

THE GEOLOGIC ORIGIN OF THE GULF AND ITS ISLANDS

I'm out early on the ship's aft deck watching a full moon set behind the striking escarpment of the Sierra de la Giganta. As the sun begins to peek above the horizon behind me, the multi-hued cliff bands of the sierra ignite into shades of pink, salmon, green, and gold. From the ship, the layered rocks look similar to the walls of the Grand Canyon, but their geologic histories couldn't be more different. Arizona's great canyon is primarily composed of sedimentary beds laid down in shallow warm seas, swamps, river deltas, or petrified wind-blown dunes. The Baja rocks are the result of much more violent and heated events.

About 250 million years ago, long before there was a Gulf of California, long before mammals ruled the earth, even before the dinosaurs were the dominant life-form, there was one huge continent—Pangaea. As the Mesozoic began (230 million years ago), Pangaea began to break apart, the Atlantic Ocean opened, and the North American continent began to move westward, pushing against the thinner oceanic crust of the Pacific Ocean. By 150 million years ago, a section of the eastern Pacific Ocean floor, the Guadalupe Plate (part of the much larger Farallon Plate), began to slide under the west coast of Mexico—the process of subduction. At the same time, the plate was being added to by magma from the earth's mantle oozing upward along its western margin—an ocean-spreading zone called the East Pacific Rise.

Immense friction along the subduction zone of the oceanic and the continental plates melted their edges, but also metamorphosed some of the pre-existing rocks and sediments. The resulting magma tried to rise

FIGURE 5   Magma melted its way vertically up and through the surrounding volcanic tuff, then cooled and hardened into a resistant dike, whose parallel edges are now exposed due to erosion.

toward the surface, but in places cooled while still deeply buried. The relatively slow cooling allowed large crystals of quartz, hornblende, and other minerals to grow into huge batholiths, or masses, of granites and diorites.

Magma that did reach the surface either exploded upon the landscape as pyroclastic (literally, fiery chunks) material or flowed out as lava. Composite volcanoes (composed of a variety of igneous rocks), shield volcanoes (composed of successive lava flows), and cinder cones (primarily composed of pyroclastics) stacked up, resulting in a volcanic island arc off the west coast of North America. Pressure from the pushing together of the plates "wrinkled" their edges into high mountain ranges along the coast. For a hundred million years, this continued until the Guadalupe Plate was consumed, along with much of the Eastern Pacific Rise.

During the Paleogene (65 to 23 million years ago), the uplifted coastal mountains were slowly eroded down into a gently rolling surface, exposing the older underlying batholithic granites and diorites. Large rivers meandered across this landscape, carrying the eroded sediments from Arizona down to Sonora and the Pacific Ocean.

Though surface eruptions had ceased, rumblings deep underground continued. Between 25 and 11 million years ago, what was left of the East Pacific Rise rotated clockwise relative to mainland Mexico and began to wrench the continent's edge apart. Slowly, the western margin of Mexico was stretched. The crust began to fracture into long, somewhat parallel faults. One of the major breaks is today's infamous San Andreas Fault. Great slices of the west coast began to slide northward. Some of this unstable real estate rotated between faults, forming block-fault mountains, which typically have steep cliffs on one face and a gentler slope on the opposite side. This stretching and faulting allowed some land to subside below sea level and ocean water to invade.

By the beginning of the Neogene (ca. 23 million years ago), as rifting continued, renewed eruptions sent volcanic ash and pyroclastics high into the atmosphere, only to fall back to earth, sometimes settling in rivers, the ocean, or into lakes, or sometimes on dry land. If still hot enough, the volcanic ash welded into tuff or angular pieces of volcanic rock mixed with ash solidified into breccias. If cool, the ash and rocks collected into deposits that could later be cemented together by

FIGURE 6   Tuffs, which are consolidated volcanic ash, are the predominant rock on many of the Midriff Islands, such as Isla San Francisco.

mineralized groundwater (volcani-clastic sediments). This widespread volcanic activity continued for almost 20 million years before settling down to occasional, localized eruptions. The thousands of feet of thickness of volcanic rock and the thousands of square miles of coverage of the volcanic activity in Baja and northwest Mexico make the 1980 eruption of Mount St. Helens in the Pacific Northwest look like a mere geologic hiccup. It is these deposits that are now exposed in the Sierra de la Giganta cliffs and many of the nearby islands.

Remember that up to the Neogene, even though sections of the west coast were sliding around and in places being uplifted while other parts were subsiding, overall these pieces were still part of the North American Plate. In the early part of the Neogene (ca. 20 million years ago), a few islands may have existed, which would become part of the peninsula, but most of the future peninsula was under the sea, still attached to the rest of Mexico. Around 11 million years ago, what was to become the bulk of the peninsula became attached to the East Pacific Plate (that part of the ocean floor to the west of the East Pacific Rise). A million years

FIGURE 7 This cliff shows layers of tan volcanic tuff that have been tilted, with dark gray gabbro dikes running through it.

FIGURE 8 As basalt lava cools, it sometimes produces columnar jointing such as in this spectacular hundred-foot-high cliff on Isla Partida Norte.

later, much of the northern half of the peninsula was lifted above sea level, parts of the southern half were uplifted to become islands, and the Cape Region was an island (or several islands) farther south.

Around 5.5 to 4 million years ago, the plate movements accelerated. Many of the "west coast slices" now, somehow, became attached to the East Pacific Plate. Seafloor spreading (rifting) began in earnest. The present Sea of Cortez began forming, eventually extending northward into Southern California and eastward into Arizona. Some geologists believe that at this time the Cape Region island(s) became attached to the southern part of the peninsula. Continuing uplift of Southern California's mountains created the Imperial Valley, but the build-up of the Colorado River Delta cut off this northern part of the gulf. This cut-off part of the sea eventually evaporated, but was refilled with freshwater during the wet periods of the Pleistocene, only to go dry again about 10,000 years ago. A flooding Colorado River breached man-made dikes in 1905, refilling the low-lying sink and creating the current Salton Sea. By the late Pliocene into the Quaternary (ca. 3 million years ago to 2 million years ago), all the pieces began to coalesce, and the northern part re-joined the continent into the narrow, 800-mile-long Baja California peninsula.

Presently, the entire peninsula continues to move northwesterly, primarily along the San Andreas Fault, "racing" along in a geologic sense at an average of a couple inches per year. Someday, the northern end of the peninsula plus part of Southern California may detach from North America, and Baja may become the island envisioned by the Spanish sailors of old.

While this rifting was (and is) going on, old Vulcan continued menacing the landscape. At the head of the gulf is the impressive lunarscape of the Pinacate Volcanic Field, containing more than four hundred cinder cones, ten enormous maar craters created by great steam explosions, and vast flows of jagged aa and ropy pa-hoe-hoe basalt; none of these igneous features are more than 1.7 million years old. This unworldly place has served as a training ground for astronauts before they blasted off to the moon. The Pinacate volcanics abut the Gran Desierto, the largest area of drifting golden sand dunes, some with stellar shapes, in North America. This giant sandbox is filled with sediments primarily derived from the ancient Colorado River Delta.

FIGURE 9   Sunset glow on the rim of a maar crater, a crater believed to be
formed by an explosion of steam, within the Pinacate Biosphere Reserve.

On the peninsula, north of Santa Rosalía, are the Tres Vírgenes, tall
volcanoes overlooking more basaltic lava outpourings, where an eruption was reported in 1746. Supposedly, one of the Vírgenes smoked
in 1857.

When I am leading a geology walk and pointing out various rocks
and minerals, I like to mention the most common rock found in this
area. It's called leaverite. Leave it right there. We practice the ethic of
Take Only Photos and Leave No Trace.

So now you know a little about the origin of the rocks making up the
region, but what about the islands themselves? During times of maximum glaciations (there were no glaciers locally, but much of the planet's
waters were frozen at higher latitudes, lowering sea levels worldwide),

FIGURE 10   Isla Smith (Coronado) is made up of layers of volcanic tuffs and other igneous rocks. Erosion has given it its conical, volcano-like shape.

islands currently separated by a depth of less than approximately 450 feet were connected to the peninsula or mainland.

A few, such as Isla Ángel de la Guarda, are, in a sense, remnants of the peninsula left behind as Baja continues on its journey. However, it is a bit more complicated than just having a peninsula piece break off and stick to the sea floor. Many of the islands are elongated, with shorelines roughly parallel to the axis of the gulf: clear evidence of their origin as uplifted blocks along faults.

Other islands have formed through volcanic eruptions from sea-floor vents, which in turn are related to the rifting of the sea floor and the creation of new sea floor. Eruptions continue until the layers of basalt and other igneous material stack up, finally breaking the surface of the sea.

Studying the origin of this enigmatic sea, its islands, and the "rafting" peninsula is helping to bring together what were once perceived

FIGURE 11   Volcanic tuff can vary greatly in hardness and color depending on its specific mineral composition, such as here at Playa de la Ballena, Isla Espíritu Santo.

as isolated geologic problems. For instance, the role that the timing of the gulf's formation plays in the geologic history of the Grand Canyon to the north is now recognized. Geologists have, and still are, pondering the exact age of that magnificent hole in the ground in northern Arizona. Deciphering what was going on geologically in the gulf helps unravel the geologic story of the Grand Canyon.

Of course, concomitant with all this geomorphologic and physiographic evolution were climatic changes. Since the mid-Paleogene (ca. 40 million years ago), there has been an overall drying trend in this part of the world. In mid-Pliocene times (ca. 3 million years ago), the Cape Region was a lush tropical forest with crocodiles, green iguanas, boa constrictors, semi-aquatic elephants, giant hares, and large cats. During the Pleistocene (ca. 2 million to 12,000 years ago), intermittent glacial periods brought abundant moisture, along with lower temperatures. Interglacial times were warm and dry, encouraging wooded grasslands to replace the tropical environment and to become home to horses and giant tortoises. Some of the interglacials were no doubt warm and dry enough to allow conditions similar to our modern desert ones, only to retreat when ice age climates returned.

The present Sonoran Desert began to form about 9,000 years ago, with the current assemblage of plants and animals achieved about 4,500 years ago. The increasing aridity was due in part to the uplifting of the peninsular mountain ranges, which created a rain shadow over the gulf. The areal extent of the Sonoran Desert waxed and waned with alternating wet and dry climatic phases from the late Pliocene through the Pleistocene to the present. During this long geologic time period, fauna and flora from the more tropical areas mixed with the temperate ones. When the climate was wet, certain species from both regions could survive here. When conditions dried, mesic-loving plants and animals usually had to retreat. A few, such as snails, occasionally found refuge at isolated springs, seeps, or other mesic micro-habitats. Their distribution was more widespread during wet periods, but now they are restricted to relatively moist locales.

Much of the evidence for past environmental changes and determination of the makeup of past plant communities comes from the pollen and plant parts found in ancient packrat middens. The same midden or

FIGURE 12 Cetacean fossils, like this imbedded whale vertebra from Isla San José, may help shed light on the evolution of whales.

nest sites are sometimes used for thousands of years by countless generations of rats. Some of the oldest middens studied so far are nearly fifty thousand years old! The packrats collect stems, leaves, and bark to add to their midden. As the rats urinate and defecate in their nest, the plant material and wind-blown pollen becomes stuck in the waste, which eventually hardens into a shiny, varnish-like material called amberat. Paleobotanists study ancient plant parts to date various layers of the amberat and re-create past plant assemblages. Midden records suggest that distribution of xerophytes (arid-adapted plants) remained fairly constant during maximum glaciations, but the ranges of mesophytes (moisture-adapted plants) expanded and contracted with changing climates.

As mentioned earlier, the Sonoran Desert receives its paltry few inches of precipitation during two different times of the year. During the winter, cyclonic systems bring moisture from the north Pacific. These storms usually cover a broad area with gentle rains. In the summer, moisture from the Gulf of Mexico moves west, and thunderstorms are the rule. These summer rains are often scattered, but can be locally heavy downpours.

The islands in the gulf, however, miss most of the winter storms' precipitation, but are subjected to strong, drying winds, the infamous Los Nortes. Instead, the gulf receives most of its moisture from the summer thunderstorms and from hurricanes in the fall that usually are born off the west coast of central and southern Mexico. Instead of heading west out to sea, an occasional hurricane may track up the gulf, dumping prodigious amounts of rain and leading to severe flooding.

Periodically, tropical storms form within the gulf: these are known as *chubascos* and can be as dangerous as any hurricane. They may last only a few hours, but torrential rain and high winds can cause severe damage. In spite of these potential sources for moisture, the gulf, particularly the northern end, is on average one of the driest parts of North America, receiving less than three inches per year.

Summer temperatures are brutal, with afternoon highs exceeding 115 degrees Fahrenheit in the shade. Ground exposed to the midday sun may be a scorching 180 degrees or more—one hellish place to live. But winters are mild, with temperatures rarely falling to freezing—a delightful time to visit.

Finding appropriate landing sites on these desert islands, especially for our city-dwelling shipmates, can be challenging. But Isla Tortuga, named for its turtle-like profile—a classic shield volcano—called to us one fine day. A small beach looked promising. We lowered the Zodiacs off our ship and motored to the island. However, once on shore, we quickly encountered aa—craggy mounds of basalt. Traversing the lava was difficult for us naturalists and definitely treacherous for our guests. Loud buzzing coming from several hidden endemic Isla Tortuga rattlesnakes (*Crotalus tortugensis*) was also unsettling. Further exploration would have to wait for another day.

Tortuga is one of the fifteen or so major oceanic islands in the gulf, meaning that it emerged from the sea after the gulf formed. Most of the other islands are land bridge (continental) islands; they were once part of the mainland and/or peninsula. Usually, islands that are relatively close to a mainland are land bridge islands, and oceanic islands are quite far away, but in the gulf this generalization does not hold. For instance, Isla Ángel de la Guarda is a mere ten miles off the coast of the peninsula, but is separated from it by the mile-deep Canal de las Ballenas. Such a deep trench so close to shore suggests significant vertical displacement along faults on the sea bottom, making Ángel an oceanic island.

The land bridge islands do tend to be young—no more than fifteen thousand years old—and they have been created by rising sea levels, subsiding land, erosion, or a combination of all three. A few are islands only at high tide—Islas Willard and Requesón being two examples.

The islands' geology—whether it's the case-hardened tuff looking like dripping, melted wax on Isla Espíritu Santo; or the celery green tuff on Isla San Francisco, whose color is a result of super-hot water altering its physical character; or the dark gray dikes of gabbro slicing through the salt-and-pepper diorite on Isla Santa Catalina; or the fruitcake medley of textures and color in towering cliffs on Isla Ángel de la Guarda—is an endless source of amazement to me. Trying to unravel the islands' geologic history and identify the multitude of rocks and minerals is a never-ending challenge. As one geologist friend likes to say, "Geology is the foundation of everything." And here in the Sea of Cortez, understanding the geologic history helps explain the evolution of the landscape and its inhabitants.

GEOLOGIC TIME

Recently, the International Commission on Stratigraphy reorganized some of the geologic time periods. Here is their latest classification.

Cenozoic era (65 Ma* to present)

Paleogene period (65 Ma to 23 Ma)
  Paleocene epoch (65 Ma to 58 Ma)
  Eocene epoch (58 Ma to 38 Ma)
  Oligocene epoch (38 Ma to 23 Ma)
Neogene period (23 Ma to 2 Ma)
  Miocene epoch (23 Ma to 5 Ma)
  Pliocene epoch (5 Ma to 2 Ma)
Quaternary period (2 Ma to present)
  Pleistocene epoch (2 Ma to 10,000 years ago)
  Holocene epoch (10,000 years ago to present)

* Ma = millions of years ago

2

Lessons *from* Anak Krakatoa

AN INTRODUCTION TO ISLAND BIOGEOGRAPHY

One of the most persistent mysteries about islands is how their complements of plants and animals arrived. To begin to unravel this puzzle, let's journey halfway around the world from Mexico to an obscure volcanic island in the Sunda Strait between Java and Sumatra. During the sultry tropical summer of 1883, the island of Krakatoa began to rumble sporadically.

On the afternoon of August 26, Krakatoa's restlessness turned terrifyingly violent. Throughout that evening and night, loud detonations and flashes of brilliant light punctuated the dark. The next morning, the entire island exploded with a deafening roar, and most of it disappeared. The noise was heard three thousand miles away on the island of Rodrigues, and more than five cubic miles of fine volcanic dust and igneous rubble were blasted into the stratosphere, twenty miles above the surface of the earth. The amount of solar radiation reaching the lower atmosphere was decreased by 20 percent during the next year by the dust veil, which produced magnificent sunsets and lowered worldwide temperatures for several years, causing crops failures as far away as New England. Krakatoa had been located just north of the Java Trench, a subduction zone similar to the one in Baja's early geologic history.

All was quiet for nearly a half-century, but in June 1927, small submarine eruptions began to rock the submerged caldera. After six months of steaming, spurts of ash, and bombs of pumice, cones of water sixty feet high shot into the air and then black magma shot even higher. The eruptions grew in strength. One day, dangerous huge jets of yellow flame pierced the surface. Finally, on January 26, 1928, a small, humped, scimitar-shaped island began to take form above sea level. It didn't last long. The surf wore it away in several weeks. But more explosions followed—sometimes a startling 10,000 to 14,000 in one day—building a second island, which also eroded and blasted itself into oblivion within weeks. A third island broke the surface in the spring of 1930, only to explode itself to pieces. However, by mid-August, enormous amounts of magma began to accumulate, a process that continues to the present, creating a fourth version of the island. Appropriately, it is called Anak Krakatoa, or "Child of Krakatoa," one of the youngest islands in the world.

Biologists became interested in the return of life to the remains of Krakatoa—now three small islands, all sections of the original caldera rim, named Rakata, Panjang, and Sertung—and the rebirth of life on its new offspring. Initially, scientists assumed that Anak Krakatoa and the remnants of Krakatoa were completely sterile, an assumption that has since been challenged.

Unfortunately, there were precious little pre-eruption data on the flora and fauna living on Krakatoa. In an attempt to ascertain the various species, botanists have studied a sketch made by John Webber, a member of the Captain James Cook expedition that paused there in 1780. Palms and ferns are definitely depicted. A few scientists visited the island in the eighteenth and nineteenth centuries, collecting a few grasses, pepper plants, orchids, mahogany trees, an unusual parasitic mistletoe, and five types of snails—hardly a definitive list. A particular type of grass re-appeared on the volcano remnants in 1920, a palm tree (*Licuala spinosa*) in 1982, and a type of fern in 1987.

One of the first scientists to reach Rakata, a mere six weeks after the fiery blast, was Dutch geologist Rogier Verbeek, but he was too early. The ground was hot, and mud flows were still pouring from lava cliffs. Six months later, Belgian biologist Edmond Cotteau discovered a tiny spider spinning its web among the gray rocks. How did this first terrestrial inhabitant reach the island? Ballooning, perhaps? Some spiders can spin strands of silk; wind currents then catch these strands and carry them off to new destinations.

Within months, the rush of life returning to the three island remnants was impressive. An expedition to Rakata in June 1886 found 15 species of flowering plants, 2 mosses, and 11 ferns. On top of the volcanic ash was a gelatinous layer of blue green algae (which are cyanobacteria, a bacterium with the ability to photosynthesize like green plants). Within twenty-five years, there were at least 114 species of plants and 263 species of animals, including 4 land snails, 2 reptiles, and 16 birds. By 1923, forty years later, 621 species of animals were living on Rakata, including a twenty-foot reticulated python, a reptile known to be a powerful swimmer, which probably arrived by swimming from the mainland.

Even though more than a century has passed, the diversity of species on these islands is distinctly different from either Java or Sumatra, the nearest sources of terrestrial organisms. Perhaps the island environment is still evolving (e.g., the soil is still too volcanically new), and reaching the island and then surviving may be impossible for many species. Then there is the controversy, dubbed by botanists as the Krakatoa Problem, as to whether or not any living thing survived the terrific 1883 blast.

There is no doubt that Anak Krakatoa was initially sterile, with the remote possibility that some sort of chemolithoautotrophic hyperthermophilic archaebacteria, a very primitive form of bacteria with a ridiculously long but descriptive name, may have been brought up from deep sulfurous vents, but none have been found on the island. This island was a perfect natural laboratory to study the arrival of life. Unfortunately, biologists were slow in visiting. Not until fifty years later did research begin in earnest; visiting the area is still hazardous because of frequent ash falls and fresh lava flows.

From this classic island biogeography story, let's now return to the Sea of Cortez. As discussed in the geology chapter, islands can be classified as land bridge (continental) or oceanic. A land bridge island was once part of a larger land mass that became disconnected either through tectonic movements or rising sea levels (sometimes combined with subsidence and/or erosion). Most of the Gulf of California's islands are land bridge types, including the gulf's largest island, Isla Tiburón. Oceanic islands are either the emergent summits of volcanoes and their attendant lava flows or sea floor faulted upward. Isla Ángel de la Guarda and many of the smaller Midriff Islands to its southeast are oceanic. Farther south, Islas Tortuga, Monserrat, Santa Catalina, Santa Cruz, San Diego, and Cerralvo are also oceanic.

Before Charles Darwin and other scientists began to shake up our perceptions of the antiquity and dynamism of the earth, many people assumed that plants and animals were simply placed where we find them by God at the beginning of creation. However, biologists have some different ideas. They have identified six main types of colonization.

One of the easiest ways for plants and animals to be on an island is when the island was once part of the mainland. During the last maximum glaciations, which ended about 12,000 years ago, sea levels may have been up to 450 feet lower, and some of today's islands were connected to mainland Mexico or the Baja Peninsula. As the sea level rose, already-established plant and animal communities became isolated on those land bridge islands. One example is the desert mule deer (*Odocoileus hemionus*) found on Isla San José.

A second way of reaching an island is to fly or swim there. Of course, birds, bats, and many insects simply do that. Some animals are good swimmers, although saltwater may present a challenge.

A third scenario is called rafting or waif dispersal. At first, it may be hard to imagine plants and animals reaching a remote island via a rafting mass of vegetation. However, according to biologist Allan Schoenherr's *A Natural History of California*, every thirty to fifty years major floods wash significant amounts of material from North America's coast out to sea. For example, in 1955, a black-tailed jackrabbit was found on a kelp raft some thirty-nine miles off Southern California's shore. Other possible rafting examples are the Isla Carmen whiptail lizard (*Cnemidophorus carmenensis*) and the Isla Monserrat whiptail lizard (*C. pictus*), which are sister species (i.e., derived from a common ancestor species). Since Isla Carmen is a land bridge island, once connected to the peninsula, herpetologists believe that its whiptail lizard population came from the peninsula. However, Isla Monserrat is an oceanic island, so they think that its whiptail population originated through overwater dispersal from Carmen. Carmen's topography suggests this possibility—the island has a thousand-foot-high mountain range, and storm runoff from its slopes has formed a large deltaic fan that faces toward Monserrat, only a twelve-mile float away.

A fourth way to reach an island is through air flotation. Small insects, spiders with web parachutes, and certain seeds can be blown many miles by wind currents. For example, in the fall of 2002, Southern Californians saw clouds of ballooning spiders wafting onshore from the sea.

A fifth possibility is via passive transport. Tiny eggs and seeds can become stuck on the feet or in the feathers of birds who visit the islands. Also, ingested seeds may not be digested, and the bird will excrete them.

A sixth possibility is by vicariant transport. This refers to plate tectonics. Herpetologists, upon examining the distribution of reptiles around the gulf, have theorized that at least two groups of reptiles are found where they are today through tectonic events during the Miocene and then later in the Pliocene. Before the acceptance of plate tectonics, the Baja Peninsula and Sea of Cortez were believed to have been in situ for many millions of years. Therefore, the modern reptile population on the peninsula probably had to come from Mexico by going around the head of the gulf. However, the idea that the peninsula is essentially a part of mainland Mexico that broke off and "rafted" to its present position led herpetologists to theorize that maybe the reptiles and amphibians were simply passengers on this raft. But as geologists unravel more about the tectonic history of Baja, herp distribution is definitely more complicated than that. One mystery is that the land that would become the peninsula appears to have been under the sea before breaking off from the mainland. So exactly how did reptiles reach the emerging peninsula? Yet another challenging question for biologists to answer.

To these six scenarios, I would add a seventh one, which until relatively recently was underappreciated by biologists—that of human activity, either accidental or deliberate. Agave is one example of this. In the past, Sonoran Desert Native Americans derived up to 50 percent of their food from agaves in the spring. Thus, the current distribution and density of this very important plant have been altered by human harvesting and husbandry. Animals, too, were sometimes moved around. The Seri claim to have transplanted chuckwallas to Isla Alcatraz from Isla San Esteban, presumably to provide a future emergency food supply.

Consider also the case of the Second Harvest. The Cochimí feasted on the ripe pitahaya fruit, defecating in a specific location. Like all cactus fruits, these fruits contained numerous small seeds. The Indians would carefully pick through the feces, gathering the seeds to be ground into a flour meal—an activity called the Second Harvest. Not all of the seeds would be recovered, so wherever feces were left, new cactus plants had the possibility to germinate.

Then there are "camp followers." The small seeds of edible plants such as Watson's amaranth (*Amaranthus watsonii*) and nettleleaf goosefoot (*Chenopodium murale*) can easily hitchhike their way to new locations when stuck to bodies or clothing. Also, some animals, like geckos, can stow away on a boat, which may explain the peculiar distribution of leaf-toed geckos (*Phyllodactylus* spp.) throughout the Midriff Islands. The species on Isla Partida Norte seems to be derived from mainland Sonora; however, the geckos on the surrounding islands appear to be from the peninsula. Aboriginal seafarers in balsa canoes may have inadvertently transported a few individuals around the gulf.

When we visit the islands on our cruises, we try to practice the ethic of Leave No Trace and hopefully no stowaways either. But even the best intentions can go awry. Sometimes guests wander off by themselves to enjoy the solitude and quiet of the place.

On one Lindblad Expeditions trip, we had returned from a particularly isolated island, heaved anchor, and sailed off into the proverbial sunset. Several hours had passed when a passenger mentioned that he had not seen his wife for awhile. Over the loudspeaker, the missing woman was paged and paged again. No response. Our only conclusion was that she must be back on the island.

The captain turned the ship around and steamed toward our last island. By now it was dark, but as the ship drew close to shore, the captain trained the ship's bright spotlight along the shore, and there she was, the missing woman, much relieved. The ship employed a tag board to keep track of everyone: when you left, you took your tag; when you returned, you replaced the tag on the board. The woman had not taken her tag, but I don't think she wanted to colonize the island.

Reaching an island is still no guarantee that a creature or plant is going to survive and reproduce. There may not be suitable habitat and/or there may be competition for resources. On the other hand, a remote island may have few competitors, increasing the probable success of the new immigrant.

Despite these challenges, the islands of the gulf contain about 695 species of plants, which is close to 20 percent of the species for the Sonoran Desert as a whole. Perhaps not surprising, almost half of those species can be found on Isla Tiburón, the gulf's largest island and only a mile from mainland Mexico.

FIGURE 13   Giant barrel cactus, cardón, and pitahaya are some of the common desert plants on Isla Santa Catalina. Offshore are a Lindblad Expeditions cruise ship, a private boat, and a Mexican fishing boat.

Islands continue to fascinate biologists. Naturalist David Quammen emphasizes, "Islands give clarity to evolution . . . [islands] serve as Dick-and-Jane primers of evolutionary biology, helping scientists master enough vocabulary and grammar to begin to comprehend the more complex prose of the mainlands." We all know how instructive Charles Darwin's voyage to the Galápagos Islands turned out to be.

Back in the 1960s, ecologists Robert H. MacArthur and Edward O. Wilson wrote *The Theory of Island Biogeography*. In this groundbreaking treatise, they proposed that there are two basic factors that influence the number of species on an island. They wrote that the rates of immigration are balanced by the rates of extinction. In other words, when the number of species is at its maximum, then the rates of immigration and extinction are in equilibrium. Animals with good dispersal options, such as birds, show this relationship. MacArthur and Wilson also acknowledged that the size and age of the island play roles in determining the number of species that can become established. Although these may seem like very reasonable and logical assumptions, more recent studies have uncovered examples of islands that do not display these concepts. For example, in the Sea of Cortez, the population densities of lizards and mammals are often greater on small islands than on larger ones.

Some of the gulf's insular plants and animals are unique endemic forms. They can be relictual endemics (those that are remnants of species formerly distributed widely) or autochthonous endemics (those that have become genetically different from the founder population). Typically, it is the more remote islands that favor the latter type. Perhaps surprisingly, there is no guarantee that a very remote island will have a large number of endemics, and being close to a source does not prevent endemism from occurring. As a matter of fact, Isla San Pedro Nolasco, which is only eight miles off the Sonoran coast, has a relatively high percentage of endemic species, including an aster (*Coreocarpus sanpedroensis*), three small cacti (*Echinocereus websterianus, Mammillaria cerralboa, M. tayloriorum*), three lizards (*Ctenosaura nolascensis, Uta nolascensis, Cnemidophorus bacatus*), and a mouse (*Peromyscus pembertoni*).

Founder individual(s) may not be representative of the gene pool. This can take evolution in a particular direction. For example, perhaps the endemic black jackrabbits (*Lepus insularis*) on Islas Partida and Espíritu Santo are the result of the founder (first) individuals being on the slightly dark side compared to the mainland population. Over many generations, this darker coloration became intensified and became the contemporary charcoal black hare.

In general, island endemics are produced when the length of time the island population has been isolated has been great. The degree to which the island environment differs biotically and physically from the founding mainland also affects the development of island endemics.

There are four primary directions endemism trends toward on islands—gigantism, dwarfism, loss of mobility, and niche shifts. Isla San Esteban has its giant pinto chuckwallas and spiny-tailed iguanas. Isla Santa Catalina has small side-blotched lizards (*U. squamata*); Isla San Pedro Mártir has its large version (*U. palmeri*). Isla Santa Catalina has the tall giant barrel cactus (*Ferocactus diguetii*); whereas, Isla Carmen has a short variety (*F.d. carmenensis*).

FIGURE 14   The giant barrel cactus (*Ferocactus diguetii*) is endemic to the Baja Peninsula and a few of the islands—Islas Carmen, Cerralvo, Danzante, Monserrat, San Diego, and Santa Catalina. Some individuals on Isla Santa Catalina are over twelve feet tall.

FIGURE 15 The colorful, speckled, endemic Isla Santa Catalina side-blotched lizard (*Uta squamata*) is one of the more attractive and smaller of the side-blotched lizards in the gulf, rarely over 2¼ inches in length from snout to vent.

FIGURE 16 The dusky Palmer's side-blotched lizard (*Uta palmeri*) is endemic to Isla San Pedro Mártir and is the largest of the side-blotched lizard species occurring in the gulf region, measuring up to 3¼ inches from snout to vent.

FIGURE 17 Little is known about the natural history of the endemic Isla Ángel de la Guarda rattlesnake (*Crotalus angelensis*) other than that it is very common on gravelly beaches as well as in rocky arroyos, washes, and hillsides. This species is up to five feet in length, nearly twice its peninsular counterpart, the speckled rattlesnake (*C. mitchellii*).

After studying island animals in Baja and around the world, biologist J. Bristol Foster made some generalizations regarding size. Foster's rule states that rodents tend toward gigantism, carnivores tend toward dwarfism, and artiodactyls (even-toed ungulates) usually tend toward dwarfism. Another way of putting it is that small mainland animals tend to get bigger on islands and big mainland animals tend to get smaller.

But rules are made to be broken, or at least bent. On the Baja Peninsula lives the red diamond rattlesnake (*Crotalus ruber*), which is about twice the size of the speckled rattlesnake (*C. mitchellii*). However, on Isla Ángel de la Guarda, the opposite is true. Ecologist Ted Case hypothesizes that the speckled rattlesnake may have colonized the island first, evolved toward gigantism, and filled the "big rattlesnake niche" before the red diamond rattlesnake arrived. Herpetologist L. Lee Grismer reports that because of the abundance and huge size of this giant rattlesnake, up to five feet in length and quite stout, Mexican fishermen do not camp on Ángel. (Recently, herpetologists have reclassified the large form of *C. mitchellii* as an endemic species called *C. angelensis*. But Case's general idea may still be correct.)

Loss of mobility can apply to animals (e.g., flightless birds) or to plants, where the mechanism for wind dispersal is lost when plumes of seeds disappear and seeds become larger.

One example of niche shift is when there are fewer competing species, and a resident organism can occur in greater abundance. This can also lead to adaptive radiation: "unfilled" niches are eventually occupied by new varieties or species of organisms. Probably the most famous instance is Darwin's finches on the Galápagos Islands, where an ancestral finch evolved into at least thirteen species, each with its own specific niche requirements. No doubt there are examples of adaptive radiation on the gulf islands just awaiting discovery.

3

Mexico's Galápagos

ISLAND LIFE

The amount of time the Sea of Cortez islands have been isolated ranges from several million years ago, such as in the case of Isla Estanque, to less than 11,000 years ago in the cases of the land bridge islands such as Isla Carmen. When UNESCO was studying the area for World Heritage Site status, they included 244 islands and islets of the 922 counted by the Mexican Comisión Nacional de Áreas Naturales Protegidas.

The plant and animal species living on the desert islands are delightfully diverse, including sea lions, Sally Lightfoot crabs, iguanas, boobies, tropicbirds, and a land tortoise. The Galápagos have their counterparts. Endemic and relict populations are some of the fascinating things about life on these islands.

In the Sea of Cortez, botanists recognize about twenty-eight insular plant endemics. About half belong to the cactus family, those remarkable truculent succulents, ranging from tennis ball–sized pincushion cacti to the towering and massive cardón.

Pitahaya dulce or organ pipe cacti (*Stenocereus thurberi*), with their tall, slender, columnar arms reaching skyward, are common and distinctive. When they bloom in late spring to early summer, the southern long-nosed bats (*Leptonycteris curosoae*) come to lap up the cream-colored flowers' nectar. Pallid bats (*Antrozous pallidus*) swoop in to feed on noctuid moths that have also arrived for a sweet drink. In the desert heat, some of the nectar ferments, and fruit flies and bees drink until drunk, then fall in and drown. The native people would also feast on the fruit of this cactus and its close relative, the tart pitahaya agria

FIGURE 18　The Sally Lightfoot crab (*Grapsus grapsus*) is found from the Sea of Cortez to the Galápagos Islands and is thought to have been named for a sultry nightclub dancer from Guayaquil, Ecuador, whose alluring performances in her red and yellow dress captivated nineteenth-century sailors.

FIGURE 19　Cardón, palo blanco, and other desert plants can be practically smothered by various types of vines after a rare wet winter storm.

(*S. gummosus*). Pulp not consumed was laid out in the sun to dry for later use: the original fruit leather snack. And recall the Second Harvest mentioned in the previous chapter. Eighteenth-century Loreto priest Miguel del Barco praised the fruit as "... worthy of being on the table of the greatest of kings." The fruit are still gathered and eaten raw and used in various food items, such as ice cream.

Most of the Sonoran Desert trees are legumes. Mesquite, catclaw acacia, smoke tree, palo verde, palo blanco, and ironwood are the common species; they are helpful in fixing nitrogen from the atmosphere into the soil, where it benefits the growth of other plants.

There are also plenty of shrubs and small trees from the torchwood and sumac families. These plants are typically deciduous and aromatic. Copal (*Bursera hindsiana*), torote colorado (*B. microphylla*), and torote blanco (*Pachycormus discolor*) are common species. The ephemeral wildflowers, bursting upon the scene after an infrequent rain, are mostly from the sunflower family.

THE DELTA ISLANDS

In 1922, conservationist great Aldo Leopold, along with his brother Carl, made a canoe trip to the Colorado River Delta. As they paddled along, they found a delta covered by "a hundred green lagoons"; water meandering through "awesome jungles" of willows, mesquite, and cottonwood; and "a river reluctant to lose its freedom to the sea." Scores of egrets, cormorants, geese, avocets, willets, yellowlegs, teal, mallards, and widgeon lurked in the bosque. The brothers came across the spoor of mule deer, raccoons, bobcat, coyote, and searched for the rumored *el tigre*, or jaguar. Sandhill cranes bugled overhead, doves cooed, and Gambel's quail mournfully called. Mullet and other fish cruised the waters. In the past, Cucupa Indians lived off its bounty and farmed panicgrass (*Panicum sonorum*) along the banks. But only fourteen years after Leopold's visit, Hoover Dam was completed, and the Colorado River and its delta were irrevocably changed. Additional dams and diversion projects have robbed the river's flow. There is no longer an expanding and renewing river delta. Instead, there are three thousand square miles of mostly salt-encrusted mudflats. Today, depending upon tidal flows and whether or not any Colorado River water is reaching the gulf, there may be at

FIGURE 20
The Midriff Islands provide nesting grounds for about 50 percent of the world's blue-footed boobies, with Isla San Pedro Mártir possibly having the largest colony in the world. Some years, biologists have recorded at least 110,000 breeding pairs on this one island.

the river's mouth three flat muddy islands—Gore, Pelícano, and Montague—and various sandbars. The great galleries of trees are gone, and the remaining plant diversity is about a third of the original.

UPPER GULF ISLANDS

Isla Rocas Consag, named for Padre Fernando Consag, who explored the west shore of the gulf all the way to the Colorado River Delta in 1746, looks like a ghostly sailing ship floating about twenty miles east of San Felipe. Unlike its extrusive volcanic neighbors to the south, it is a chunk of Cretaceous granite that was brought to the surface through faulting and is now liberally coated with bird guano. Few, if any, vascular plants grow on Rocas Consag, but it is home to many sea birds, including brown pelicans, boobies, gulls, and cormorants.

FIGURE 21   Brown boobies lay their eggs on skimpy, precarious cliff ledges on tiny Los Islotes off the north end of Isla Partida Sur.

The remaining half-dozen or so upper gulf islands are clustered no more than a few miles offshore southeast of Puertecitos. This is an area of frequent mirages, leading some folks to call them the Enchanted Islands. They are composed primarily of Miocene-age extrusive volcanic rocks. The geology of Isla San Luis is especially interesting. The island consists of several low ridges of gray pumice with a dark dome of obsidian, or volcanic glass. On the south end of the island is a maar, a crater formed by an explosion of steam.

MIDRIFF ISLANDS

The Midriff Islands region contains about fifteen major islands, including the two largest ones in the gulf—Isla Tiburón, which is also Mexico's largest island, and Isla Ángel de la Guarda, Mexico's longest.

The imposing Isla Ángel de la Guarda is the second largest of the gulf islands, about fifty miles long and ranging from three to twelve miles in width. It may have become an island about a million years ago as the peninsula continued its "rafting" to the northwest and faulting thrust seafloor deposits above sea level. Running the length of its northwest–southeast orientation is a two- to over four-thousand-foot-high spine of colorful igneous and metamorphic rocks, intruded with veins of quartz and diorite. Much of Ángel is overlain by thick layers of volcanic flows, breccias, tuffs, sandstone conglomerates, and fanglomerates (alluvial fan deposits that have become cemented into solid rock)—an amateur geologist's nightmare, but a fascinating puzzle to the professional.

Along several stretches of the island's coastline are broad bajadas prickling with Sonoran Desert plants. Other parts of the coast rise precipitously out of the sea with occasional breaks in the cliffs teasing the explorer. An intrepid climber might find near the island summits and high north slopes a few specimens of one of the strangest plants in the Sonoran Desert—the cirio or boojum (*Fouquieria columnaris*). *Cirio* is Spanish for the long, tapered candles used in Mexican churches. The plant's other common name, boojum, came about when explorer Godfrey Sykes from the Desert Botanical Laboratory in Tucson, Arizona, encountered the plant in 1922. He was reminded of a character in Lewis Carroll's nonsense poem *The Hunting of the Snark* that was ". . . something strange that lived in faraway places." Upon espying the plants,

FIGURE 22   In some of the larger canyons or arroyos on Isla Ángel de la Guarda grow Mexican blue palms (*Erythea armata*) [pictured here], which are endemic to Baja and some of the larger gulf islands, or Mexican fan palms (*Washingtonia robusta*), which are endemic to Baja and Sonora.

Sykes exclaimed, "Ho, ho, a boojum, definitely a boojum!" And the name stuck.

The cirio looks a little like an upside-down carrot, albeit giant and grayish instead of tiny and orange, poking out of the ground and reaching into the dry, clear sky maybe fifty or sixty feet. Sometimes cirios branch, although the ones on Ángel tend to be less treelike. One botanist has reported that cirios have an odor that resembles a mixture of carrot and ginger, musty and sweet. The cirio would seem to exhibit a perfect biogeographical example for drifting continents (or more technically and prosaically correct, vicariant transport). This odd plant is found growing only from the southern end of the Sierra de San Pedro Mártir to the Sierra Las Vírgenes on the peninsula, on Ángel at about 4,300 feet above sea level, and along a short piece of mainland Sonora coast between Puerto Libertad and El Desemboque de los Seris. Push the peninsula east back against Ángel, then continue pushing until all is reattached to mainland Mexico, and an argument can be made that in the distant past there was one cirio "forest," but then Baja split off and began to drift to the northwest. Along its journey, Ángel broke off and was left behind. And that's how the three separate populations came to be. Nice story, but not likely.

The formation of the peninsula and the island probably precedes the origin of modern cirios. But even if this species did exist prior to the breakup, its distribution was probably different than today because of climatic change. Today's distribution is possibly a good example of island colonization (this includes Baja, which, although not an island surrounded by ocean, is geographically isolated from the mainland). Cirios produce great quantities of small, winged seeds that could have been blown easily across the gulf during a *chubasco*, or hurricane.

Another possibility is that the strange plants were deliberately planted in new areas by people. Ethnobotanists have suggested and demonstrated that early desert people occasionally re-distributed plants and animals that were of economic and/or spiritual importance to them. Or

FIGURE 23   To the Seri, the strange, endemic boojum or cirio (*Fouquieria columnaris*) are giants who were overtaken by floodwaters. The tall ones were men, and the short fat ones were pregnant women. The Seri also say that to touch or harm a cirio will bring on strong winds and rain.

maybe the Seri have the correct explanation: A long time ago, giants from the south tried to escape a great flood, but the angry waters overtook them and turned the giants into the odd plants.

The boojum is essentially a succulent ocotillo (*F. splendens*), a widespread Sonoran plant. It differs from its close relative in being a winter grower. Earlier work by botanist Robert Humphrey of the University of Arizona suggested that boojums grow only a few inches a year and that the tallest ones were up to seven hundred years old. But a more recent study indicates that their life spans may typically be a century or so. Every few decades, a given boojum population experiences a direct hit from a hurricane. Tall, shallow-rooted boojum, cardón, and senita are especially vulnerable to high winds, and these plant populations suffer significant losses of large individuals from these events.

The tallest known boojum was discovered by Humphrey in Montevideo Canyon near Bahía de Los Ángeles in the 1970s; at the time it was 81 feet tall. In 2002, this giant boojum was measured again at about 81–82 feet tall, with no apparent change in twenty years. An adjacent cardón looked nearly the same except for a single two-foot-long new arm on one of its many stems. Growth can be very slow in the desert.

While cirios are pollinated by a large number of insects, Steven Buchmann and colleagues at the Carl Hayden Bee Research Center in Tucson, Arizona, discovered that in each of twenty years of a study, there was a very different array of species collected in the same boojum populations in Baja California and Sonora. Many species were not seen again for several years. These pollinators may be another example of temporal niche separation. The boojums flower every year, but different insect pollinators emerge in different years in response to as yet unknown environmental cues.

During my first season working aboard the Lindblad Expeditions cruise ship in the Sea of Cortez, arrangements had been made to visit the boojum forest above Bahía de Los Ángeles on the peninsula. The bay does not have a dock suitable for a ship, so we anchored offshore and took Zodiacs in.

On shore we were greeted by entrepreneur and local legend Antero (Papa) Diaz and a motley collection of old rusted trucks and vans to take our group up into the mountains. The road had been paved at one time, but was now mainly a series of potholes held together with patches of blacktop. Nonetheless, we made it to the boojums and delighted in photographing their weird and wonderful shapes in the late-afternoon light.

Upon return to the bay, we were shuttled into Papa and Cruz (Mama) Diaz's restaurant for a very special dinner. The National Audubon Society had chartered our ship for this particular cruise, thus the passengers were presumably staunch defenders of wildlife, especially endangered species. Unfortunately, Papa Diaz had decided that for his dinner guests, turtle soup would be ideal. Guests were horrified, and our trip leader was totally embarrassed. A few of us poked our spoons at the chunks of turtle meat floating in our bowls, and I must admit that the soup was delicious. We quickly moved on to the next course of fish tacos and refried beans. Needless to say, future meals at the Diaz restaurant were carefully planned ahead.

To the southeast of Ángel is Isla Tiburón—at about 464 square miles not only the largest of the islands in the Sea of Cortez but also the largest island on the Pacific coast of North America south of Canada. Two mountain ranges, the Sierra Kunkaak and Sierra Menor, trend north–south and are separated by the Agua Dulce Valley. The highest peak is nearly four thousand feet. Tiburón is also one of the few islands that once supported a sizeable human population (the Seri), possible in part because it is the only Midriff island with permanent springs.

Along Tiburón's coast is littoral scrub habitat, greatly influenced by tide and salt spray. To survive here, plants must be very salt tolerant. Inland, Sonoran Desert vegetation is the rule. Tree cacti such as cardón, pitahaya dulce, senita, and a few saguaros on ridges are mixed with elephant tree, creosotebush, ocotillo, palo verde, ironwood, brittlebush, and jojoba. Along the arroyos and washes, where there is occasionally a little more moisture, is a riparian habitat composed of palo blanco, sweet bush, mesquite, desert lavender, and bursage. At the higher elevations, the riparian species are in denser concentrations.

One brief bird survey in the 1960s by biologist Roland Wauer found 105 species on Tiburón, of which 38 were breeding. The rest were migrants or winter residents. The most common breeder was the tiny verdin, second was the California gnatcatcher, followed by the black-throated sparrow, white-winged dove, ash-throated flycatcher, Costa's hummingbird, and cactus wren. Just these seven species accounted for about 60 percent of all the birds breeding on the island.

FIGURE 24 These smooth, grayish-white barked trees (*Pachycormus discolor*) on Isla Ángel de la Guarda belong to one of several unrelated tree species commonly called elephant trees because of their elephant trunk–like branches. This particular species is endemic to the Baja Peninsula and some of the northern to Midriff Islands.

Other animals on Tiburón include coyotes, mule deer, and introduced desert bighorn sheep. Cattle, goats, hogs, and pronghorn antelope were released over the last century or so, but have been removed or died out. Tiburón also has a native tortoise (*Gopherus agassizii*).

Off the north coast of Tiburón is a tiny, rocky outcrop called Isla Patos. This was one of the first of the gulf islands to be mined for its guano. Although the mining operation was disruptive to nesting birds, the native birds returned once mining ceased in the early 1900s. Around 1945 or 1946, Peruvian cormorants were introduced in the belief that they could quickly replenish the guano and revive the mining industry, but the imported birds died off. Today, upwards of fifty thousand pairs of brown pelicans nest here and slowly contribute more guano.

An 1896 *National Geographic Magazine* article by W. J. McGee and Willard D. Johnson warned that Isla Tiburón and the adjacent coast was the "fatherland of a fierce tribe, the terror of explorers since Coronado,

FIGURE 25   This female Costa's hummingbird, the most common hummingbird encountered on the islands, is incubating two tiny white eggs in a nest made of plant fiber and down. The eggs will hatch in a little over two weeks, and the chicks will fledge after about three weeks.

FIGURE 26   The Midriff Islands provide nesting habitat for about 50 percent of the world's California brown pelicans. Their population (as well as those of osprey, bald eagle, and other fish-eating birds) crashed in the 1960s and 1970s as a result of contamination by insecticides, but the banning of DDT has resulted in recovery in many areas.

the dread of Sonora today, the nightmare of the few settlers." But one March day found my wife Ann, our young daughter Kate, and myself bouncing down a washboard gravel road heading north from Bahía Kino to visit these alleged "fierce" people.

By the 1960s, most of the Seri had left the island to live in two Sonoran coast villages. As we neared one of these villages, *federales* stopped us at a roadblock. A plane carrying illegal drugs had crashed close by, and the feds were checking all vehicles passing through. After a quick and efficient search of our car, we were allowed to continue on our way.

I steered into the village of Punta Chueca and stopped the car. Dozens of Seri swarmed around us. It was a little intimidating, especially as they pressed forward with unsmiling, penetrating eyes staring right through us. But as we got out of the car, we realized that what they wanted was to sell us baskets and snail-shell necklaces, and they were curious why these gringos had driven way out to their village.

For untold centuries, the Seri had managed to be self-sufficient hunters and gatherers living off the unpredictable resources of the Sonoran Desert, surviving the vagaries of the sea on meager amounts of freshwater. They had somehow discovered the secret of winter-sleeping green turtles (*Chelonia mydas*) on the ocean floor—a behavior not known to science until 1976. Unfortunately, Mexican fishermen had also discovered the hibernating turtles by the 1970s and, within a decade, had depleted the population. To the Seri, this was a land of plenty. Only to our "civilized" eyes is it a land devoid of sustenance.

A few miles southwest of Isla Tiburón, Isla San Esteban rears out of the sea. Until the late 1800s, a small, enigmatic band of the Seri called the Coftécöl Comcáac, literally "chuckwallas-large-people," lived here. Considered to be great seafarers by the other Seri, they crossed the dangerous channels in reedgrass (*Phragmites australis*) balsa canoes. According to anthropologist Thomas Bowen, who has spent decades studying and exploring the island, the San Esteban people apparently had no knowledge of the bow and arrow, did not wear much clothing, slept without blankets, knew essentially nothing of the outside world, and spoke in a sing-song manner. What eventually became of these people is not clear. They may have perished at the hands of Mexican soldiers.

The first time I landed on Isla San Esteban, the sun was barely breaking the eastern horizon. On the small pebbly beach was a Mexican fishermen's camp. The fishermen were no doubt baffled by this early-morning landing of middle-aged turistas. We explained that we were in search of the giant lizards, the pinto chuckwalla (*Sauromalus varius*) and the spiny-tailed iguana (*Ctenosaura conspicuosa*), that lived here. Both species can attain lengths of two feet or more. At that, the fishermen laughed, pointed up a broad arroyo, and said, "Sí, sí. Allí hay muchas iguanas." And off we went. When it was time to return to the ship, we came back to the same beach to wait for the Zodiacs and discovered a very large chuckwalla being roasted over a campfire by our fishermen amigos. Tastes like chicken?

Besides these giant lizards, the Seri have a legend about crocodiles (*Crocodylus acutus*) once inhabiting Islas San Esteban and San Lorenzo. However, biologists point out that this cannot be true from a physiological point of view: this species of crocodile cannot survive crossing seawater. Today, there are crocs on the mainland in the El Fuerte River in northern Sinaloa. And in 1973, a two-meter-long crocodile was captured in Las Guasimas, about eighteen miles southeast of Guaymas. But crocs on the islands? Not likely. Eighteenth-century Catholic missionary John Jacob Baegert wrote a fanciful account of crocodiles living at the Colorado River Delta in 1751. However, he never actually visited the Colorado, so his report is not credible, either.

On succeeding visits to San Esteban, I often hike up this same arroyo, Arroyo Limantour, to watch the stocky iguanas and chuckwallas emerge from their nocturnal hiding places and slowly climb into cardóns to feed on the cactus flowers. A mile or so up the arroyo are some deep pits dug into the soil and rows of boulders arranged into rough rectangles. After years of wondering about the mysterious stone arrangements, I was leading yet another hike up to the site when I spied several people walking down the arroyo. We stopped to say howdy and chat. One of the hikers was Tom Bowen. He knew the secret to the enigmatically arranged rocks. They were "drying racks," and the pits were "baking ovens." Mexicans had come to the island in the 1870s to harvest agaves to make mezcal liquor. Agave expert Howard Scott Gentry noted that mezcal is to tequila what moonshine is to whiskey. Since there was no freshwater locally to mix with the baked agave hearts, the cooked plants were laid on rocks out of the dirt to cool and dry. The dried agave hearts were then transported to the mainland for final processing into fiery liquor.

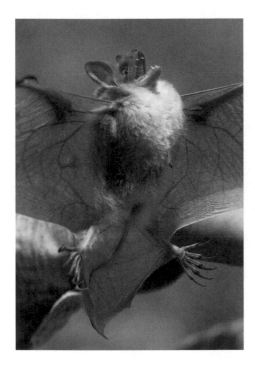

FIGURE 28 Scientists believe that fish-eating bats (*Myotis vivesi*) can detect slight ripples on the ocean's surface made by fish, swooping down and snagging a fish using their long, sharp claws. Fishing-eating bats occur only in the Sea of Cortez area and a small area along the west coast of Baja.

Between Ángel and Tiburón are about a half-dozen small islands, each one biologically fascinating. Isla Partida Norte is composed of columnar basalt cliffs and slopes of volcanic boulders. The island harbors fish-eating bats (*Myotis vivesi*) and least and black storm-petrels. Both the bats and birds roost under rocks in tiny burrows. Fish-eating bats range throughout the gulf, but seem to be restricted to certain rockslide habitats for breeding. They have long legs and toes tipped with lethal claws for picking small fish off the ocean surface. If a bat is late in returning from its nighttime foray, gulls and peregrine falcons are known to attack them.

This island is also home to the endemic night snake (*Hypsiglena gularis*). Most people don't realize that night snakes are poisonous, probably

FIGURE 27 This species of spiny-tailed iguana (*Ctenosaura conspicuosa*) is known only from Isla San Esteban and nearby Isla Cholludo. Adults are often seen perched on the top of cardóns (*Pachycereus pringlei*), munching on the cactus flowers.

FIGURE 29   A gopher snake (*Pituophis vertebralis*), such as this one on Isla San José, can do a fairly convincing imitation of a rattlesnake when frightened by flattening its head to make it look more triangular and shaking its tail. However, these snakes lack fangs and are not poisonous; they kill their prey, primarily small mammals and birds, by constriction.

because unlike rattlesnakes, these snakes do not possess anterior fangs. Night snakes must clamp down on their prey and chew with their grooved hind teeth to allow the mildly toxic venom to be ground into the hapless creature. Humans generally don't put up with this behavior.

A few miles south of Partida Norte is Isla Rasa. As a topographic feature, Isla Rasa is unremarkable, but aptly lives up to its name, which means "flat." It is composed of Pleistocene- and Holocene-age basalt lava flows with less than one square mile of it barely protruding above the sea. Most of the rock is covered in guano. Back in the nineteenth century, guano mining was carried out here on a truly industrial scale, which had a tremendously detrimental impact on the nesting birds. Fortunately, the intensive mining ended about 1900, allowing birds to return to the island.

Puncturing the mix of rock and guano are a few scrawny cardóns and a couple of patches of cholla, and several hundred human-made stone cairns and long low walls. Presumably they were built by the miners,

FIGURE 30 Heermann's gulls are shown setting up nesting sites on Isla Rasa. Eventually, there will be about 230,000 gulls vying for space.

maybe to make the collection of guano easier, but their exact purpose is a mystery.

Come here in the spring, and almost half a million birds will be attempting to nest on this tiny island. The first to arrive are Heermann's gulls, who have flown from all along the Pacific coast from southern Canada to southern Mexico. They arrive in dense flocks, pick out their tiny plots, and almost immediately lay eggs. About ten days later, elegant and royal terns arrive, having come from as far south as Central and South America or from the California coast. They linger around the perimeter of the island as each day their numbers increase. The birds grow restless, and flocks of thousands rise, swoop low over the valleys, and return screaming to the lagoons.

Then a night comes when a tern flock numbering thousands of individuals descends on the land already claimed by the gulls. Through sheer numbers, they dispossess the gulls and start laying their own eggs. By dawn the terns control a plot perhaps fifty feet in diameter, with the

FIGURE 31   Flocks of thousands of elegant and royal terns swoop over nesting Heermann's gulls. At the height of breeding, there will be about 200,000 elegant terns and 14,000 royal terns.

evicted gulls circling the new colony and stealing any unprotected tern eggs on the periphery. Due to predation, the colony shrinks, but with darkness, additional terns arrive and the colony expands.

Shrinkage and expansion continue. By the time growth stops, the gull eggs laid first, now in the center of an acre or two of terns, begin to hatch. The precocious young band together and move through those adults that are still incubating and hide in the rocks, where they are miraculously found and cared for by their parents. The hollow center of the colony is invaded by the predaceous gulls.

During the height of the breeding season, as many as 230,000 Heermann's gulls, 200,000 elegant terns, and 14,000 royal terns are on Rasa. The ballet flight of thousands of birds is hypnotizing; the noise deafening; and the smell of guano permeating. It is estimated that Isla Rasa provides nesting habitat for 95 percent of the North American populations of Heermann's gulls and elegant terns. An additional eighty species of birds have been recorded on this tiny island.

FIGURE 32   Elegant terns flying over Isla Rasa.

FIGURE 33   Each spring, nearly a quarter-million Heermann's gulls nest on tiny Isla Rasa.

Though the big guano mining operation ceased, other activities threatened the island and its birds. Lew Walker, director of the Arizona-Sonora Desert Museum, first visited Isla Rasa in 1946. In Bahía de Los Ángeles he hired a boat "homemade from flotsam of the Gulf" and its turtle-fishing owners to take him to the island. The boat, "powered by currents, oars, and a sail full of holes," arrived at the island a day and a half later. The bounty of birds electrified Walker. Upon his return to the United States, he wrote an article with photographs, "Sea Birds of Isla Raza [sic], Baja California" for *National Geographic Magazine*. The next year, he returned to the island and, to his amazement, found very few nesting birds. The birds' absence was a puzzle, but human footprints were plentiful.

In 1948, Walker tried to return to Isla Rasa, but a terrible storm blew up, and his party took shelter on Isla Cardonosa. During the night their small boat sank, immersing cameras, supplies, and motor. They managed to raise the boat and, after three days, were successful in getting the motor running. They watched flocks of birds heading to Isla Rasa, but could not reach the island, so they finally returned to Bahía de Los Ángeles.

The mystery of the 1947 footprints and lack of birds was later explained when Walker met a Mexican fisherman who reported that people had visited Isla Rasa earlier that year to remove thousands of eggs to be sold for food in Santa Rosalía and other ports. Some minor egging had been conducted in other years, but as transportation became easier and markets grew, the eggers increased in number. Men invaded the island during the nesting season, relentlessly sweeping up the eggs, which were tested in buckets of saltwater. Eggs that floated were partially incubated and thrown away. Those that sank were fresh and were carefully packed to be sold for food in nearby ports.

As Walker returned to Isla Rasa year after year, he documented the astounding decrease in the bird population in direct ratio to the increase in human marauders. It appeared as though Isla Rasa's days were numbered. Walker decided that he had to do something about it. He brought influential friends—including nature writer Joseph Wood Krutch, California Academy of Sciences board member Kenneth Bechtel, Arizona-Sonora Desert Museum founder William Woodin, renowned ornithologist Roger Tory Peterson, National Audubon Society president Carl W. Buchheister, California Academy of Sciences biologist George Lindsay, and famed aviator and conservationist Charles Lindbergh—to the gulf to witness firsthand the desperate need for protection of Rasa and other islands.

In April 1964, the deteriorating situation on Isla Rasa was made impressively apparent when Buchheister returned to survey the Isla Rasa bird population. He found twenty-one men encamped on the island, seven boats anchored nearby, and expectation on the part of the eggers to take approximately four hundred thousand eggs. Buchheister wrote, "In short, these men were removing all eggs as fast as they were being laid, and from the entire island."

Not a single chick was to be found. He called it "one of the most shocking acts of human predation on wildlife that I have ever witnessed." Returning in June, he found that some of the terns had been able to nest a second time with limited reproduction, but he estimated that the nesting and reproduction of the Heermann's gulls for that season was a 99 percent failure!

At last, on May 30, 1964, Mexican president Adolfo López Mateos signed a decree that established Isla Rasa as a Migratory Waterfowl Sanctuary, a move that would ultimately lead to protection of all the islands in the Sea of Cortez.

How do these "bird islands" get established in the first place? Usually, they are the result of a location free of terrestrial predators and close to an appropriate food source. Isla Rasa is in the midst of one of the most productive oceanic regions in the world: a productivity resulting from a combination of coastal and tidal upwellings. And until the introduction of black rats and domestic mice (and man), Rasa had no terrestrial predators.

But the Rasa story doesn't end there. Mexican biologist Enriqueta Velarde and her assistants have dedicated more than thirty breeding seasons to studying the ecology of Rasa and its surroundings. One of their discoveries of major importance is the relationship between breeding success of the Hermann's gulls and the global cycle of sea-level pressure/ocean-temperature anomalies, or what we laypeople call El Niño. During strong El Niños, when warmer than usual water reaches into

FIGURE 34   Nearly every gulf island seems to have at least one pair of nesting ospreys. These fish-eating hawks have special barbed pads on the soles of their feet to help grip the slippery fish.

the Midriff Islands area, resulting in low populations of Pacific sardine (*Sardinops sagax caerulea*), northern anchovy (*Engraulis mordax*), and Pacific mackerel (*Scomber japonicus*) populations, the female gulls cannot find enough food to sustain their chicks, and almost no chicks survive. Velarde believes that her work on Rasa can also help predict commercial fishing success, which would be an obvious boon to the local fishermen.

About twenty miles south of Tiburón, and sitting equidistant between the Baja Peninsula and mainland Mexico, is one of the gulf's most isolated islands, with an ominous name—Isla San Pedro Mártir. At first appearance on a distant horizon, the island seems to be another illusive mirage. As the ship I work on nears, more detail can be made out, but the unreal whiteness of the vertical cliffs against the dark seawater enhances the strangeness of this place. Through binoculars, I can make out the ruins of rock buildings and platforms, remnants of a once-thriving guano industry. As the ship gets even closer, a cacophony fills the air. Boobies, both blue-footed and brown, by the thousands call with hollow whistles and squawks; red-billed tropicbirds scream and wave their streamer tails to woo a mate; and California sea lions bark and growl at each other before diving into the water and swimming under our bow. Brown pelicans take to the air, looking like squadrons of ancient pterodactyls. Thousand-foot-high cliffs soar out of the sea, the cliffs and slopes coated with smelly, chalky bird guano. The summit of the island is bristling with cardón. And then we are assaulted by thousands of tiny annoying *bobitos* (*Paraleucopis mexicana*) flying around our eyes and ears—flies that don't bite but, as one naturalist put it, "feed on anxiety and desperation."

Back in the "old days," when we didn't know any better, we naturalists would occasionally go ashore on Mártir—which can be tricky because you land on a meager rock shelf—and take our ship guests up a steep, rocky, slimy, guano-encrusted path to get a close look at the breeding boobies. The wife of a very wealthy international industrialist was on one of these excursions. She turned out for our scramble decked out from head to toe in a gold lamé jumpsuit. On her feet were gold, smooth-soled slippers. Was she trying to outshine the birds? Once on shore, she slid and slipped her way up the slope, we naturalists taking turns holding her hand or arm so she didn't tumble into the sea, where I'm sure a hungry bull shark would have been quickly attracted by such a shiny lure. By the time she returned to the ship, her outfit was liberally splattered with white guano and smelled just grand.

Another season, we lowered the Zodiacs for a circumnavigation of this mile-square rock. Besides the usual nesting boobies and king-sized endemic Palmer's side-blotched lizards hunting guano-loving flies and feeding on broken eggs and dropped fish parts, there were people staying on the island. Research biologist Bernie Tershy, at the time a graduate student, and several other biology students and researchers were living on Mártir to study the breeding birds and other resident animals, such as the disquietingly numerous western diamondback rattlesnakes (*Crotalus atrox*). I noticed that the scientists had Band-Aids and tape on their fingers. "What happened?"

Tershy replied, "Oh, at night when we are asleep, rats come into camp and bite us." Now there's dedication, or were they trying to be martyrs?

FIGURE 35   Pairs of red-billed tropicbirds bond through spectacular, synchronized aerial displays accompanied by strident, repetitive calls.

FIGURE 36   The handsome yellow-footed gull breeds only in the gulf, but afterwards may wander north to the Salton Sea or coastal Southern California.

The rats were not native. They were the prolific invaders of remote places and the world's cities—*Rattus rattus*, the black rat, which so stealthily climbs aboard ships and then clandestinely disembarks at the next port of call. During the next year's research season, Tershy and company brought children's inflatable plastic swimming pools to sleep in. The rats couldn't climb up the slippery sides.

Another time, rare thunderstorms struck the Midriff Islands. For hours, thick, white, mucky guano waterfalls poured off Mártir, fertilizing the sea and dampening us with a smelly mist of bird shit. What a strange, wondrous place.

SOUTHERN GULF ISLANDS

The twenty or so major southern gulf islands primarily lie off the east coast of the Baja Peninsula and stretch from northeast of Santa Rosalía to east of La Paz. Except for Isla Tortuga, they are considered to be land bridge (continental) islands. Several islands, such as Islas San Pedro Nolasco, Pájaros, and Lobos, don't follow this general pattern and are instead close to the Sonoran coastline.

Before taking guests ashore, our little ship circumnavigates Isla Danzante, the isle of dancers. When Spanish explorer Francisco de Ulloa approached the island in 1539, he saw men jumping up and down on a beach and thought they were dancing. But the name could also refer to the numerous stone hoodoos or fanciful pinnacles perched along the summit ridge. Or perhaps it comes from the squat, knobby-kneed trunks and branches of the torote and copal. I'm reminded of the pirouetting elephants and hippos in Walt Disney's *Fantasia*. On the hillside are the long, spiny stems of the palo adán, called Adam's tree because of its nakedness or lack of leaves most of the year. One stem supports a tiny, golf ball–sized Costa's hummingbird nest. The football-shaped nest of a verdin is tucked into a tangle of mesquite. A tiny California gnatcatcher nervously gleans twigs for invertebrates. As we continue up the wash, we flush several white-winged doves. An old desert maxim states that a lost traveler can follow doves to water, but how do you know if the doves are going to or coming from a water source? A black-throated sparrow calls from the top of a cardón with no concern about locating a desert oasis. This is the only bird of the North American deserts that never has to drink water nor get moisture from a succulent insect. The bird gets all the water it requires by metabolizing the fats and carbohydrates found in seeds.

Isla Danzante is also home to many reptiles. At first, you notice only a thin black-and-white-striped stick waving slowly back and forth. And then, flash, the "stick" speeds away, attached to a barely perceptible light brown body—this is the zebratail lizard (*Callisaurus draconoides*). If a predator should be distracted and grab the lizard's tail, it breaks off along built-in fracture planes in the vertebrae. The lizard grows a new tail, although the replacement is shorter and has a different appearance.

Our ship turns southeast to head toward Isla Santa Catalina. Once there, I take a group of ship passengers for a nature walk. I go only a hundred yards up the sandy wash when I notice a small snake slither closer to the trunk of a cardón. The reptile's mottled tan pattern blends very well with the granitic sand; only its movement disclosed its presence. I approach slowly, in part not wanting to scare the snake away, in part because I know that it is a rattlesnake, but no ordinary rattlesnake. It is shaking its tail tip violently, but no telltale buzz is heard, for this is the unique, endemic rattleless rattlesnake (*Crotalus catalinensis*) of Isla Santa Catalina, known in Spanish as *víbora sorda* (literally "deaf viper").

Why has this species lost its ability to grow rattles, and how did snakes ever reach this remote island? Baja reptile expert L. Lee Grismer theorizes that the inability to grow rattles may be an adaptation involving stealth, which would allow the snake to crawl into the lower branches of shrubs at night in search of sleeping birds to eat. Rattleless rattlesnakes are very adept climbers, having been observed up to twelve feet off the ground. Grismer notes that these snakes also have teeth that are longer than those of other rattlesnakes and thus advantageous for biting through feathers.

Rattlesnakes are not enthusiastic swimmers, especially when it comes to fifteen miles of seawater between here and the peninsula. How did the ancestors of *C. catalinensis* arrive? Rafting perhaps?

Although only about 7.5 miles long and 2 miles wide, remote Isla Santa Catalina is a biological gem, harboring a relatively large number of unique plants and animals. Although I have never come upon freshwater here, this island is home to a wide array of terrestrial desert birds,

FIGURE 37   The endemic rattleless rattlesnake (*Crotalus catalinensis*), found only on Isla Santa Catalina, is an agile climber and hunts birds and other animals perched in trees and shrubs. For unknown reasons, some of the snakes are brown, while others are ashy gray.

which have to drink or eat succulent vegetation. Walking up the sandy arroyo lined with cardóns, pitahaya, barrel cacti, palo verde, and what we facetiously call dog-turd acacia (*Pithecellobium confine*), referring to its odd-looking pods, in the late afternoon of a spring day is a great way to observe the flash of a crimson northern cardinal or the undulating flight of a ladder-backed woodpecker, loggerhead shrike, northern mockingbird, black-throated sparrow, ash-throated flycatcher, Costa's hummingbird, or white-winged dove; maybe hear a great horned owl hoot, the laughing call of mating white-throated swifts, or the descending song of the canyon wren; or see a tiny verdin diving into its football-shaped nest perched in a spiny palo adán, a nervous California gnatcatcher, violet-green swallows swishing past a cliff, or turkey vultures wheeling high overhead. This desert is anything but deserted.

This is also the home of the giant barrel cactus. The pre-eminent Baja biologist George Lindsay and his wife Gerry are pictured in Norman C. Robert's *Baja California Plant Field Guide* standing next to a fine, tall specimen of giant barrel. Years later, when George Lindsay passed away, this particular cactus also died. Two giants sadly gone.

The giant barrel cactus, the stout cardón, the palo adán, and many other of the desert's perennial plants are classified as cadophylls—a plant with no leaves for photosynthesis. So where is the chlorophyll? It's in the green stem. Loss of water from evaporation is greatly reduced by eliminating leaves or by just having them seasonally. Cacti further conserve water by conducting crassulacean acid metabolism, which is discussed in an earlier chapter.

Of all the bizarre plants in Baja, one that I find very strange looking is the endemic melón de coyote (*Ibervillea insularis*). Most of the year it resembles the rounded, salt-and-pepper granite boulders that it grows among. For a long time, I never noticed these weird plants. In winter, after a particularly heavy *chubasco* season, the extra moisture stimulates the half-buried, tuberous root to produce long, delicate vines that crawl up and over cardóns and trees and shrubs before exploding with tender green flowers. After a few weeks, red or yellowish bitter fruits appear. Then the vines die and eventually decay, and the cement-like tuber is all that remains until the next wet season.

Besides an endemic cottontail rabbit (*Sylvilagus mansuetus*), the large, mountainous Isla San José has an endemic kangaroo rat (*Dipodomys merriami insularis*) and spiny pocket mouse (*Chaetodipus spinatus bryanti*), two of the small desert rodents that never have to drink water or eat succulent food. Like the black-throated sparrow, these mammals manage quite nicely by utilizing water produced through the metabolism of fats and carbohydrates found in dry seeds, avoiding the heat of the day, having extremely efficient kidneys, and possessing a labyrinthine nasal passageway, where water vapor coming from the lungs is reabsorbed.

Until recently, the San José kangaroo rat was thought to be extinct, a victim of feral cat predation. But after fifteen years of searching and live-trapping, the rodent was rediscovered.

The land bridge islands Islas Partida Sur and Espíritu Santo lie immediately north of La Paz and at low tide almost become one island. They have steep east-facing cliffs and gently dipping westward slopes—in profile, mimicking the topography and geology of this region of the Baja Peninsula. They have been cut off from the peninsula since the end of the Pleistocene, probably through a combination of rising sea levels and erosion of what was the interconnecting land. Their relatively large size and a few sources of freshwater allow for a greater diversity of plants and animals than many of the more remote islands. They harbor nineteen species of reptiles, including one endemic lizard, Espíritu Santo whiptail (*Cnemidophorus espiritensis*), and one endemic snake, Espíritu Santo striped racer (*Masticophis barbouri*); two amphibians, the red-spotted toad (*Bufo punctatus*) and Couch's spadefoot toad (*Scaphiopus couchii*); and six mammals (not including bats), two of which are endemics, the black jackrabbit (*Lepus insularis*) and island antelope squirrel (*Ammospermophilus insularis*).

The island antelope squirrel is essentially identical to the peninsular form. But should you happen to examine its teeth, you would find that more than half of the island squirrels are missing one or both of their premolars. Biologists wonder if there is an ecological significance to this or if it is an example of genetic drift. Antelope squirrels are one of the few desert mammals that can be active during the heat of the day. They partially shade themselves by holding their bushy tails up and over their backs, which is equivalent to moving into a shady spot that is 11 to 14 degrees F cooler. Since the squirrels neither sweat nor pant, they lick their fur for evaporative cooling. They will also spread their bodies against shaded ground to transfer heat at a rate of about one degree per minute.

Having black fur may seem disadvantageous for the jackrabbit, but radiant heat is absorbed by the hair and doesn't reach the skin as easily as a lighter color would allow. Think about other dark-colored, diurnal animals of the desert, such as common ravens and turkey vultures. Their black feathers also prevent some of the sun's energy from reaching their skin.

A Couch's spadefoot toad can metamorphose from egg to tadpole to toad at the lightning-fast rate of eight days. Not a bad adaptation for a desert-dwelling amphibian, where pools of rainwater dry up quickly. As their aquatic home shrinks, some of the tadpoles die, and their decaying bodies release chemicals that stimulate the remaining tadpoles to metamorphose even faster. Once transformed into an adult, and after snacking for a few days on invertebrates, the toad, using the sickle-shaped black spade on each of its hind feet, digs a hole to escape the desert's aridity and to wait for a future rain. If the tadpoles lose the race to adult-hood as the puddle dries up, then their dead bodies shrivel into what one biologist wisecracks are desert raisins.

In hopes of observing a black jackrabbit or antelope squirrel or one of the endemic reptiles on Isla Espíritu Santo, I enter the rocky canyon behind the island's bay known as Ensenada Grande. I pass a massive pile of old, weathered oyster shells—a prehistoric midden—clear evidence that people, probably the Pericú, once came here to fish for oysters. Carbon dating documents that oyster fishing has been going on here for at least the last seven thousand years. I continue up the drainage, which reveals several surprisingly undesert-like plants. One is the rock fig (*Ficus palmeri*), with broad shiny leaves and tiny dry fruit (which one botanical wag quipped are "eaten by birds and children for no apparent reason"), its pale, sensuous trunk clasping at the cliff like an octopus. The other is the gorgeous endemic passionflower vine (*Passiflora arida* var. *cerralbensis*) climbing over shrubs. Its fruit is claimed to be an aph-rodisiac. Both of these plants are reminders that some of the Sonoran Desert flora is derived from tropical or semi-tropical ancestors.

By boulder-hopping up the drainage, most of the sharp, thorny plants can be avoided, but I still arrive at the head of the canyon with trickles of blood running down my bare legs. Near the top of the island are single rows of small rocks, presumably tiny windbreaks for ancient "bedrooms." Whoever slept here had a breathtaking view down the nearly sheer east face of the island.

Besides the more obvious wildlife, such as seabirds, land birds, and reptiles, there are many species of invertebrates to be found on the gulf islands: ants being one of the most common island residents. There are about sixty-five species known from the gulf islands. A larger island such as Isla Ángel de la Guarda is home to over two dozen species, but some islands have only one or two native species. Four or five species seem to be island endemics, but this status may change as more research is done on the Mexican mainland and Baja Peninsula. At least one non-native ant (*Paratrechina longicornis*) has colonized islands in Bahía de Los Ángeles and off Loreto, presumably introduced by human transport.

Sometimes as I stroll up a desert wash, I encounter a little black beetle trundling along. If I poke at him, he may stop, raise his rear end,

FIGURE 38 There are about five hundred species of passionflower in tropical and subtropical regions of the Western Hemisphere, mostly in South America, but only four species occur in the Baja California area. This species (*Passiflora arida* var. *cerralbensis*) is endemic to Baja and a few gulf islands.

FIGURE 39 This spectacular flower belongs to a mistletoe (*Phrygilanthus sonorae*) that parasitizes torote colorado (*Bursera microphylla*) and other shrubs on Isla Santa Catalina.

and possibly emit a foul-smelling gas. In English, he is called a stink bug (although really a beetle, not a Hemiptera or true bug); in Spanish, he is called *pinacate* (derived from the Aztec word for black beetle) and belongs to the Tenebrionid beetle family. Not all the species have the defensive gas, but they all exhibit the same "headstand" behavior when threatened. Mice that feed on these beetles will push the offensive butt-end into the ground and start eating by gnawing on the beetle's head.

The Tenebrionid beetles are one of the dominant animal groups on the gulf islands. Except for ants, these beetles account for as much as 70 percent of the ground arthropod fauna. There are 103 species inhabiting at least sixty-six of the islands; 25 of the species are endemics and 1 is an endemic genus. Not a bad representation for a little creature that goes around farting. Why are so many of the islands inhabited by Tenebrionids? One reason may be that the flightless species have fused elytra (outer wings). Air pockets under the elytra allow for additional buoyancy so that the beetles raft well. Being omnivorous is helpful too, since once they arrive at an island, they can take advantage of the limited food resources.

LIFE AT THE ISLAND'S EDGE

The land and sea intertidal zone, or more eloquently, the land between the tides, or more prosaically, the lower part of the beach, is a fascinating habitat, an excellent example of edge effect. Because it retains characteristics of both ocean and terrestrial habitats, it is home to organisms associated with both regions. Thus, diversity of species within ten vertical feet in the intertidal zone is typically greater than in any other habitat on earth.

The first serious collector of marine organisms in the Sea of Cortez was a U.S. government tidal observer named John Xantus, who was stationed at the southern tip of the Baja Peninsula from 1859 until 1861. But the first wide-ranging biological expedition wasn't until 1940, led by biologist Ed Ricketts and his close friend, writer John Steinbeck, aboard the purse seiner, the *Western Flyer*. Their pioneering work is chronicled in the famous classic *The Log from the Sea of Cortez*. Although many additional surveys have

FIGURE 40 Magnificent frigate birds spend days and nights on the wing, with an average ground speed of about 6 miles per hour, covering as much as 250 miles before landing. They alternately climb in thermals, to altitudes occasionally as high as a mile and a half, and descend to the sea surface to perhaps snatch a fish near the surface.

been conducted, gulf invertebrate expert Richard Brusca estimates that at least half of the marine species (mostly invertebrates) still remain scientifically undescribed, while the natural history of almost all of them is unknown.

Many, if not most, of the islands' intertidal zones are rocky. Clamped tightly onto rocks are hermaphroditic barnacles. Barnacles may appear to be boring creatures, just sitting there firmly cemented to a rock, enduring whatever the sea and life throws at them. However, the sex life of barnacles borders on the lurid. Though most species are hermaphrodites, cross-fertilization is the norm, presumably more fun than self-fertilization. Unlike many marine invertebrates that simply spew eggs and sperm into the water and hope for the best, barnacles actually copulate. Which brings up the obvious question: How do these sessile creatures do it? The answer is by having a very long penis. They possess one of the most prodigious penises relative to body size of any animal, up to forty times the length of their body!

The fertilized eggs hatch into free-floating larvae, which transmogrify into a second larval form called a cypris. Ed Ricketts described the cypris as "an animal with three eyes, two shells, six pairs of legs, and an inclination to give up the roving habit of its youth and settle down."

Then there are the miniature China hat–shaped limpets, that while seemingly immobile and rigid are actually territorial—they do this by secreting chemicals that discourage other limpets from growing too close. Good secretions make good neighbors. Scampering over, around, and under the stones, rock lice (*Ligia occidentalis*) search for algal wrack to eat. Lifting up a rock may reveal tiny, fingernail-sized porcelain crabs (*Petrolisthes* spp.), or a small brittle star (*Ophionereis* spp.), or the remarkable three-quarter-inch, brown *Vaejovis littoralis* scorpion in densities of up to twelve individuals per square meter. Knowing this may give one pause about standing ankle deep in the ocean. But not to worry, the stinger on these miniscule arthropods is too small to do any harm to us monstrous humans.

However, the islands do have plenty of larger scorpions to be concerned about. The most renowned scorpion researcher in this part of the world was Gary Polis from the University of California at Davis. By using a portable ultraviolet light at night, he could locate scorpions glowing eerie neon green in the dark. Many new species were discovered this way. Polis also discovered that some of the islands contain two to twenty-five times the scorpion densities that are found on the mainland. Sadly, a few years ago, off of Isla Cabeza de Caballo, the boat Polis was riding in capsized and he drowned.

When the weather and sea conditions permit, we like to have an evening barbeque on shore for the guests and crew. It's a relaxing way to enjoy the lapping of the sea against the beach and watch a million stars slowly appear in the darkening sky. Many of our shipmates live in cities or urban areas, where light pollution obscures the Milky Way and the other celestial wonders.

Occasionally, one of the naturalists brings out a portable ultraviolet light and tries to gather a group to move from the sandy beach into the nearby desert. Once he has his unsuspecting group together, he flicks the light on. Faint, glowing, greenish yellow dots appear under cactus, on rocks, on branches. Scorpions! Scorpions are not typically aggressive, and without the aid of the ultraviolet light, most of us would never realize how many there are in the desert. However, this little demonstration usually starts a steady migration of ship guests back to the "safety" of their shipboard cabins.

On Isla Coronados, far up the beach in dry sand, are rimmed silver dollar–sized holes dug by ghost crabs (*Ocypoda* spp.). The holes may be four feet deep to reach damp sand. During the day, a mosquito or two may share the upper reaches of the burrow.

Rare in the winter but common in summer in the gulf is the dangerous Portuguese man-of-war (*Physalia physalis*). We once encountered one while snorkeling off Isla Santa Catalina. In the gulf, they are small and look like a drifting gelatinous blob with a strand or two of blue polypropylene rope trailing behind, but those tentacles contain a neurotoxin that can pack a nasty wallop. The Portuguese man-of-war is a floating hydrozoan, a colony consisting of four types of polyps. The stinging cells, or nematocysts, are the characteristic food-getting mechanisms of jellyfish and their close relatives. The nematocysts retain their potency long after an individual has been washed up along the shore, as beachcombers have discovered to their dismay and discomfort.

And on a warm summer's night, tiny flashes of light much like sparks of static electricity may "explode" just under the water's surface—the mating display of certain lusty dinoflagellates, a type of plankton. The ship's captain usually frowns on anyone swimming at night in the dark, but a warm summer evening with the possibility of bioluminescence in the water can be way too tempting.

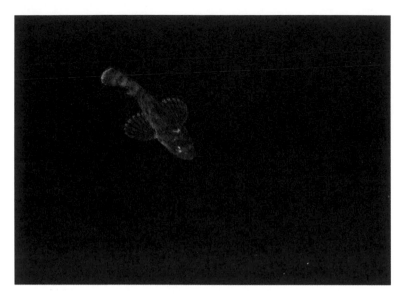

FIGURE 41 This stone scorpion fish (*Scorpaena mystes*) was seen at night near the ocean's surface, probably feeding on zooplankton, small fish, or crustaceans.

So one night after most of the ship's guests had gone to bed and the captain was off duty, several of us donned face masks and quietly slipped into the black sea for a midnight swim. Much to our delight, when we kicked or waved our arms back and forth, the water around our skin took on an eerie greenish glow. Diving under the surface, I saw my companions as ghostly lime green silhouettes. Fantastic. The harder we thrashed about, the brighter the bioluminescence became. Much too soon, we had to return to the ship. As we dripped our way back to our cabins, the night watchman gave us a knowing wink and a smile.

A waxing or waning moon can bring out the romance in fish. Little is known about the everyday life of gulf grunion (*Leuresthes sardina*), a small, silver-bodied fish that lives in the northern part of the gulf. But come spring and early summer, they gather by the thousands in the intertidal zones along sandy beaches to spawn in the surf line. This unusual fish behavior is called a "grunion run," and unlike their close relative the California grunion (*L. tenius*), which spawns only at night, the gulf grunion can run either during daylight or at night. The run is predicted by certain tides, which, of course, are controlled in part by the phases of the moon.

While beachcombing one day, I reach down to pick up an apparently dead, two-foot-long, black and yellow snake washing up on the beach, then think better of it. Good thing. It is a pelagic yellow-bellied sea snake (*Pelamis platurus*) and not dead at all, just floating with the incoming tide, probably feeding on unsuspecting small fish. They are capable of cutaneous breathing, removing oxygen from the water and releasing carbon dioxide through their skin. They are fairly helpless on land. They are not known to breed here in the gulf, requiring warm, tropical waters, so it may have drifted here on north-flowing currents. Though human deaths from the snake's venom are rare, a bite may cause lasting nerve damage.

4

Flying Card Tables
and Breaching Buses

LIFE AROUND THE ISLANDS

At first, from the bow, we just see what appears to be a darker blue line across the distant ocean horizon separating sea from sky. As our cruise ship gets closer, a binocular view reveals countless numbers of lead-gray dolphins leaping and splashing. Above the dolphins are huge flocks of pelicans, gulls, terns, and boobies wheeling around and around. Then a group of pelicans or boobies will suddenly fold their wings back and bullet into the sea to catch a fish.

Nearing the feeding frenzy, the dolphins suddenly take an interest in us, or more correctly, our ship. The captain throttles forward, knowing that our bow wave will further excite the mammals. Soon, hundreds, if not thousands, of long-beaked common dolphins (*Delphinus capensis*) (although the Lindblad Expeditions naturalists like to say that these animals are not "common," but "magnificent") have surrounded us.

Some are in front of our bow getting a free ride; others are catching air off our wake. Other dolphins launch high into the air, seemingly for the sheer joy of doing it. For many frenetic, kinetic minutes this goes on. We burn up rolls of film and fill digital photo cards until we are exhausted and camera batteries have died.

Then, without warning, as though someone blew a whistle, the churning waters calm. The dolphins line up in formation and speed away with barely a splash or ripple. We are left again on the azure blue, mirror-surfaced gulf, alone. Where did they go? And why?

During the winter in the central and southern part of the gulf, it's not uncommon to witness other marine creatures flying through the air. Occasionally, you have your basic flying fish, which are gliding more

FIGURE 42 Frenetic groups of hundreds or even thousands of long-beaked common dolphins (*Delphinus capensis*) can be encountered when sailing in the Sea of Cortez.

than flapping fins for lift. Marlin and Pacific sailfish often jump out of the water and are highly sought after by sports fishermen. But my personal favorites are the mobula rays (*Mobula* spp.), which one of our captains calls flying card tables because of their flat, table-like shape. A few years back, slow-motion movies of leaping rays revealed that sometimes the female rays expel their babies in mid-flight. What a way to start life. Usually, we will see only one or two rays at once, but occasionally there will be dozens going airborne and flipping over again and again. They can't all be giving birth, so what are they up to? One guess is that the landing splash knocks off parasites. This same flipping-over activity has been observed underwater, so it might have something to do with corralling fish into a tighter ball to be eaten. And that flying through the air part might just be accidental. But so far no one really knows.

Another spectacular jumper is the humpback whale. Not all whales attempt to be aerial, but it is a common phenomenon for humpbacks. We watched one female and her calf breach at least twenty times. Imag-

FIGURE 43 Mobula rays (*Mobula* spp.) often jump completely out of the water over and over again.

ine the amount of energy needed to push an animal the size and weight of a Greyhound bus almost totally out of the water. They emerge from the water, do a half-twist, and come crashing back down on their sides. All we could do was marvel at the spectacle.

Like the rays, no one knows for sure why these animals do this behavior. Some guesses are communication; knocking off dead skin, barnacles, and other parasites; defense; or knocking out prey.

The upper gulf marine and estuarine ecosystems rely (relied?) on the Colorado River for an influx of nutrients and freshwater. The mid- to lower gulf area receives much of its nutrients through powerful upwelling, which is controlled by seasonal winds and tidal action. Cold water carrying decaying organic matter upwells from deep submarine canyons to be "cooked" by the desert sun into a rich broth that feeds plankton. The phyto- and zooplankton in turn become the basis for the complex aquatic food chain that includes thousands of species of invertebrates, almost nine hundred species of fish, five species of sea turtles, California

FIGURE 44   It's not unusual to witness humpback whales breaching repeatedly. Some researchers believe the behavior is related to courtship or is simply play activity.

sea lions and the occasional elephant seal, a myriad of land and sea birds, and of course whales and dolphins. The Sea of Cortez is one of the world's best habitats for cetaceans. About twenty species of cetaceans live, breed, and/or migrate through these waters, including large baleen whales like blue, fin, sei, Bryde's, minke, and the largest of the toothed whales, the sperm. That is a third of the world's cetacean species.

Recently, the Interdisciplinary Center for Marine Sciences at the National Polytechnic Institute in La Paz discovered that the gulf is a prime nursery for blue whales, the largest animal ever known to exist. Blues can be nearly one hundred feet long and weigh about two tons per foot. Their tongues alone can weigh as much as an elephant and their heart as much as an automobile. A single adult consumes about four tons of krill per day: incredible that the largest animal eats one of the smallest. This is also a testament to how biologically productive the gulf waters must be.

Near the end of a chartered voyage through the gulf, we were sailing toward La Paz when a pair of cetaceans was spotted swimming toward the ship. Mexican fisheries biologist Miguel Cisneros, whale specialist and general director of the Mexican World Wildlife Fund Omar Vidal, Lindblad Expeditions naturalist Jack Swenson, and I watched the creatures swim closer and closer. Yet we couldn't identify these porpoiselike animals. Swenson raised his camera and snapped a few quick frames. The mystery cetaceans vanished under the surface.

Later, Vidal showed the pictures to Jorge Urbán, the marine mammal expert at the Autonomous University of Baja California Sur in La Paz, who was certain they were dwarf sperm whales. However, Swenson recalls, ". . . there was a sloping forehead on the mystery creature, not a domed-overhanging one like the dwarf sperm whale has." Whether it was a dwarf sperm or not or some cetacean hitherto unknown to science, this incident illustrates how the Sea of Cortez is still a huge biological puzzle awaiting solving. This is one of the wonderful aspects of this lonely sea . . . the possibility of encountering marine animals that are rarely seen.

In the spring of 2009, local people began to report another strange giant whale or fish that some dubbed The Black Demon. Some thought it might be a megalodon, a prehistoric shark, and voracious predator, presumed to be extinct for a million years. The History Channel's television show *MonsterQuest* investigated. Divers eventually identified it as a whale shark (*Rhincodon typus*), a remarkable creature indeed, but a not uncommon resident of the gulf. They are the world's largest fish, attaining lengths up to forty feet. Swimmers have nothing to fear from this placid plankton eater.

Even with whale species that are easier to identify, very little is known about their natural history. For instance, one group of cetacean scientists is trying to unravel the movements and feeding habitats of the gulf's sperm whales, the largest of all the toothed whales at lengths up to sixty feet. As Herman Melville observed in his novel *Moby-Dick* 150 years ago: "For though other species of whales find their food above water, and may be seen by man in the act of feeding, the spermaceti whale obtains his whole food in unknown zones below the surface; and only by inference is it that anyone can tell of what, precisely, that food consists."

Although the sperm whale is among the deepest divers in the ocean, routinely reaching depths of three thousand feet or more, its major prey, the jumbo or Humboldt squid (*Dosidicus gigas*), dwells closer to the surface. A mature jumbo squid can weigh more than one hundred pounds and grow more than six feet long; some have been known to attack divers in the Sea of Cortez.

In a recent study, biologist William Gilly from Stanford University and biologist Randall Davis from Texas A&M University–Galveston applied electronic tracking devices simultaneously to the deep-diving predators and their prey in the same waters. The scientists carefully approach a sperm whale and attach an electronic depth recorder to its back. Later, whenever the tagged whale surfaces for a breath of air, the device transmits recorded data about the animal's movements to an orbiting satellite.

Off of Santa Rosalía, jumbo squid are particularly abundant, with numerous small fishing boats hauling in as many as ten thousand squid per night. A few of the captured squid are outfitted with a pop-up archival transmitting tag, which periodically samples the animal's depth. Unlike the instruments used on whales, the squid tags are designed to detach at a predetermined time, then float to the surface and transmit stored data to a satellite. Tagging data showed that the whales were traveling up to sixty miles a day within a relatively small area, suggesting that they had found an abundant supply of food.

During the day, whales and squid spent about three-quarters of their time at depths ranging from 600 to 1,300 feet, which is consistent with the idea that the whales were foraging where the probability of encountering squid was highest. At night, however, the tagged squid spent at least half of their time in shallower waters above 600 feet and the remainder at 600 to 1,300 feet. One likely explanation for this vertical movement is that the squid were following small fish and other prey that migrate toward the surface at night and then return to deeper waters during the day.

Unlike squid, however, the sperm whales did not alter their diving pattern at night. Instead, they continued to spend about three-fourths of their time at depths of 600 to 1,300 feet, according to nocturnal tagging data.

Squid need a constant supply of oxygen to support their metabolism. Sperm whales, on the other hand, take oxygen down with them bound to the hemoglobin in their blood and the myoglobin in their muscles, so they don't have to worry about hypoxia at depth. By spending most of their time in cold, deep waters, sperm whales can take advantage of a vulnerable squid, whether it's slowed down by hypoxia at depth during the daytime, or at night after it has made a deep dive to escape the warm, stressful conditions at the surface.

Besides whales, the gulf is home to five of the world's seven species of marine turtles. In the past, egg laying may have been common along the beaches of the Baja Peninsula, but it is now rare and restricted to isolated beaches and remote islands. On the islands, the only terrestrial turtle is the desert tortoise. It is found on Isla Tiburón and perhaps on Isla Datíl.

Even far from shore, it's not uncommon to occasionally see a California sea lion (*Zalophus californianus*) or two leaping from the water through the air, a behavior called porpoising, or lying motionless with flippers held high like sails to gather solar heat. But one day near Isla San Pedro Mártir, we cruised near a lone pinniped. Much to our amazement, it was a lounging Guadalupe fur seal (*Arctocephalus townsendi*). Usually, this species is restricted to Isla Guadalupe on the Pacific side of Baja. What was it doing here? Looking for new habitat, or had it simply made a wrong turn at the southern tip of Baja?

Another year, another unusual sighting near Mártir was that of a California gray whale. A few enter the gulf each year instead of migrating northward along the Pacific coast of the peninsula. As our cruise ship visited this island through the winter and spring months, we would see a small gray whale swimming slowly back and forth along the base of Mártir. On each visit, the whale appeared to be thinner, and then it vanished. Was it lost? Did it eventually starve to death?

Farther north on the north side of Isla Ángel de la Guarda there is a small "colony" of northern elephant seals (*Mirounga angustirostris*). Like the fur seal and gray whale, they seem to be out of their "normal" range, which is on the Pacific coast islands. Or are they? Maybe this is one way of colonizing new areas, sometimes successfully and other times not. For now, biologists consider these individuals vagrants.

Anchoring off the southeast end of Ángel, we disembarked from our ship to explore. On the beach was a pile of hammerhead shark bodies sans dorsal fins. Shark populations in the gulf have suffered tremendously since the 1980s due to overfishing for their fins. Fins are shipped

FIGURE 45 California sea lions (*Zalophus californianus*) were hunted commercially in the gulf from the early nineteenth century until the 1960s, primarily for their oil. Although now legally protected, a few are still killed by fishermen for shark bait.

to East Asian markets, where shark fin soup is a popular dish for special occasions. It is also purported to be an aphrodisiac. SeaWatch, an organization that has chronicled this slaughter, estimates that more than two hundred thousand sharks were killed from 1985 to 1995 in the Midriff Islands area. Some scientists estimate that shark populations have diminished worldwide by more than 90 percent in the last fifty years! Nearby, an almost complete skeleton of a dolphin had washed up on the beach. Was it, too, a victim of the fishermen?

We were led down the beach by Ian McTaggert-Cowan, a distinguished zoologist from the University of British Columbia, to a shallow pond full of greenish gray algae—not a very exciting sight. But then, he announced that we were looking at living stromatolite-producing blue green algae. Still not impressed? Imagine back billions of years ago when the earth was first experimenting with something called life. The first living organisms were probably simple bacteria-like entities. By

FIGURE 46 This rare Guadalupe fur seal (*Arctocephalus townsendi*) was photographed near Isla San Pedro Mártir, far from its usual range along the west coast of Baja and its breeding grounds on Isla Guadalupe in the Pacific Ocean.

FIGURE 47 Northern elephant seals (*Mirounga angustirostris*) are typically found on islands off the Pacific coast of the Baja Peninsula and as far north as the Gulf of Alaska. But on our Lindblad Expeditions voyages, we have seen groups of young animals on the small islands near the north end of Isla Ángel de la Guarda.

2.4 billion years ago, one type was blue green algae, more technically called cyanobacteria (yes, the same type of green slime that was found on Rakata). For hundreds of millions of years, cyanobacteria and their relatives absorbed carbon dioxide out of the water and carried on photosynthesis, which produced oxygen as one of the products; some species produced calcium carbonate (limestone) as another product. The preserved limestone is called stromatolites. The oceans slowly became more and more oxygenated. Remember, too, that the earth's atmosphere during these ancient times was acidic, short on oxygen with an abundance of carbon dioxide. Approximately 540 million years ago, an oxygen-rich threshold was apparently reached, and evolution took a giant leap toward more complex organisms dependent on oxygen. Scientists refer to the seemingly quick, in geological terms, emergence of many species as the "Cambrian Explosion of Life."

Now back to our skuzzy pond. Over geologic time, most stromatolite-producing cyanobacteria went extinct. Evidence of their past existence is found as conical, stratiform, branching, domal, and columnar-shaped deposits of limestone. Today, living stromatolite-producing cyanobacteria are only known from a few locations—one being Shark Bay in Western Australia and another here on Isla Ángel de la Guarda.

UNDER THE SEA

In a sense, the submerged rocky reefs around the perimeter of an island are their own unique "island" habitats, places that are biologically distinct from the surrounding open ocean. While there are coral heads, sea fans, and other kinds of corals, most of the gulf's average winter water temperature is too cold for reef-forming corals to survive around the islands. Associated with and mostly restricted to the rocky reefs are certain species of fish and invertebrates, some that range south to the Galápagos Islands and some that are endemic to the Sea of Cortez. How these creatures

---

FIGURE 48   Although the average seawater temperature in most of the gulf is too cool for reef-forming corals, other types of corals do exist, such as these coral heads off Isla Espíritu Santo.

manage to cross open, deep water to take up residence around an island is yet another puzzling and challenging aspect of island biogeography.

To take a look at the residents of a rocky reef, I put on my face mask, snorkel, and fins and ease into the cool water off Isla Santa Catalina. The water is not crystal clear like one might see in the Caribbean, but rather a little cloudy from billions of miniscule plankton, the staple of the marine food chain. As I slowly paddle around, I am immersed in fish. There are king angelfish, Cortez damselfish, Panamic sergeant majors, Cortez rainbow wrasse, blue chromis, orangeside triggerfish, yellowtail surgeonfish, guineafowl puffers, Pacific Ocean boxfish, stinging hydroids (ouch!), crown of thorns, encrusting stony coral, robust gorgonians, brown sea fans, tan sea stars, sea urchins, and scores of other fish and invertebrates I can't identify.

While sitting in a boat or relaxing on an island beach, there are few hints to this busy ecosystem just below the sea's surface.

5

Vanishing *Vaquitas* and Burning Deserts

THREATENED ECOSYSTEMS

The Colorado and other rivers that once flowed into the gulf are now dammed and diverted, which prevents important nutrients from reaching the sea. The lack of inflowing freshwater, coupled with the high evaporation rate of the desert climate, has caused parts of the Sea of Cortez to become more saline, especially around the head of the gulf.

In those rare wet years when some water reaches the Arizona-Sonora border, the Moreles Diversion Dam allows U.S. cities and agriculture to siphon off about 95 percent of that, so only a mere 5 percent reaches Mexico. Mexican farmers use that small amount; thus, virtually no water reaches the gulf.

The Colorado River Delta area is where a Spanish galleon filled with treasure supposedly lies buried, a victim of the tidal bore; where steamboats once chugged between the sea and Yuma (although a unusually high tidal bore in September 1922 wrecked one ship, killing 130 people); where Colorado Delta clams (*Mulina coloradoensis*) were so numerous they formed entire islands; where conservationist Aldo Leopold exalted about the glorious abundance of wildlife; where mesquite, cottonwood, and willow bosques once stretched to the sea. Now the delta is mostly a dead, saline mudflat baking in the desert sun. For the last decade or so, there has been a campaign urging the American Southwest states to give up a fraction of their allocated water. A 1 percent increase in flow might restore much of the area's ecology.

The gulf's only porpoise, the *vaquita*, is endangered, too. In 1958, when whale authority Ken Norris was still just a graduate student, he found three cetacean skulls near San Felipe. He took them back to school in Berkeley and eventually realized that he had discovered a new species, a porpoise that the local Mexicans called *la vaquita*, the little cow (*Phocoena sinus*). Even after a couple of decades, no scientist was to see a vaquita in good enough condition to make an illustration for identification purposes. Not until 1987 was a live one that had been trapped in a net photographed.

The vaquita is the smallest living cetacean, weighing less than 120 pounds. It resembles the common porpoise (*P. phocoena*). The main body color is gray, darker around the eyes and mouth and on the top than on the bottom. There is a dark stripe from the chin to the base of the flipper. The vaquita prefers shallow lagoons along the shoreline, where there is strong tidal mixing and high productivity.

The vaquita appears to feed on small bottom-dwelling fish and squid; another source claims that a favorite food is the disappearing totoaba. It swims and feeds in a leisurely manner, but it is elusive and tends to avoid boats. High-frequency clicks are used for echolocation. The vaquita occurs singly or in small groups and may have formerly occurred throughout the Gulf of California. It was considered abundant in the early twentieth century, but as of the early 1980s, the only records are from the northern part of the gulf. Currently, it has the most limited distribution of any marine cetacean.

The vaquita declined starting in the 1940s, in conjunction with the intensification and modernization of commercial fisheries. The fisheries, aimed at a variety of species, are intensive in the upper Gulf of California, and the incidental trapping and drowning of vaquitas, particularly in gill and trawl nets, is their principal threat. In 1941, author John Steinbeck described a twelve-boat fleet of shrimpers who "were doing a systematic job, not only of taking every shrimp from the bottom, but every other living thing as well. They cruised slowly along in echelon with overlapping dredges, literally scraping the bottom clean." Unfortunately, sixty years later, this type of harvesting continues. At one time, two-hundred-pound totoaba (*Totoaba macdonaldi*) were the important sport and commercial fish of the upper gulf. Large schools of these bass-like, big-lipped croakers migrated to the brackish waters at the delta's mouth. But since 1975, it has become endangered.

Seasonally depleted oxygen levels are becoming a major problem in certain parts of the world's oceans, including the Sea of Cortez. The cause is nutrient over-enrichment from human sources. Excess nutrients lead to increased algal production, a process known as eutrophication.

Researchers have long suspected that fertilizer runoff from big farms can trigger sudden explosions of marine algae capable of disrupting ocean ecosystems and even producing "dead zones" in the sea. A 2005 study by Stanford University scientists Kevin Arrigo, Pamela Matson, and Mike Beman used satellite imagery to link large-scale coastal farming on the Mexican mainland to massive algal blooms in the Sea of Cortez. Harmful blooms are artificially fueled by the fertilizer runoff, which dump tons of excess nitrogen into rivers that reach the sea.

In the gulf, wind-driven upwellings regularly bring nutrients from the sea floor to the surface, stimulating the rapid reproduction and growth of microscopic phytoplankton. These algal blooms are natural events that benefit life in the gulf by generating tons of phytoplankton, a major source of food for larger organisms. But some phytoplankton species produce harmful blooms, known as red or brown tides, which release toxins in the water that can poison mollusks and fish. Excessively large blooms can also overwhelm a marine ecosystem by depleting oxygen in the water.

Immigration of plants and animals to the islands is still occurring as it has in the past. However, many of these species are not native to the Western Hemisphere, let alone the gulf. An exotic species invasion almost always spells trouble for the natives. Exotics can, and often do, outcompete the natives for space and resources. All of these new arrivals are extremely tolerant to salt and drought, are spread easily, and are further encouraged by wildfires.

One is tamarisk (*Tamarix chinensis*), a Middle East native, brought to the United States as early as the 1820s to be planted in alkaline soils for erosion control. However, one tamarisk tree can produce a half-million tiny, windblown seeds. The seeds need only a slight amount of freshwater to germinate, after which the seedlings can tolerate saltwater. Within a few decades, tamarisk spread throughout the American Southwest, becoming a major pest. I have seen it on Isla Ángel de la Guarda, and it has been reported from Isla Alcatraz, another one of the Midriff Islands.

Another troublesome species, the crystal iceplant (*Mesembryanthemum crystallinum*), has been planted as ground cover in Southern California and has moved south into Baja, including to a few islands. Unlike

FIGURE 49   Although it produces a beautiful flower, the non-native crystal iceplant (*Mesembryanthemum crystallinum*) is invading some islands and may eventually threaten native plants.

tamarisk, iceplants do not have windblown seeds, but their seeds can float, germinate, and thrive in saltwater. Another iceplant, Hottentot fig (*Carpobrotus edulis*) from South Africa, establishes new colonies by growing long runners. Once entrenched, iceplants are very difficult to eradicate.

During the 1870s, Russian thistle or tumbleweed (*Salsola tragus*) found its way from the steppes of Mongolia to North America, allegedly as seeds embedded in a shipment of flaxseed. It quickly spread throughout the West to become an icon in cowboy movies, immortalized in the song *Tumblin' Tumbleweeds*, and a scourge to be reckoned with.

African buffelgrass (*Pennisetum ciliare*) was deliberately planted in various parts of the Sonoran Desert beginning in the 1940s to be used as cattle feed. It grows fast, outcompeting native plants for the scarce water. It can then dry out and catch on fire, which kills off native cacti and shrubs, and then sprout from seeds, preventing the slower-growing native desert plants from returning. There has been an attempt to eradicate buffelgrass from Isla Tiburón, but hardy populations have been seen on other islands, such as Alcatraz. Its windblown seeds can withstand saltwater immersion, making it possible for seeds to be blown and float to islands.

Giant reed (*Arundo donax*), a native of the Mediterranean, chokes riversides and stream channels, crowds out native plants, interferes with flood control, increases fire potential, and reduces habitat for wildlife, including the least Bell's vireo, an endangered bird.

Giant reed can float miles downstream where root and stem fragments may take root and initiate new infestations. Due to its rapid growth rate and vegetative reproduction, it is able to quickly invade new areas and form pure stands at the expense of other species. Once established, giant reed has the ability to outcompete and completely suppress native vegetation. It ignites easily and can create intense fires.

Sahara mustard (*Brassica tournefortii*), a native to many areas of the Old World from North Africa and the Middle East to southern Europe and Pakistan, has invaded parts of the North American deserts, where in wet years it may totally cover the ground, creating an extreme fire hazard. It is a frightful thought that hyperarid desert, including sand dunes, can burn because of this weed. Most Sonoran Desert plants cannot tolerate fire; burned areas become wastelands of nearly pure exotic weeds.

Of animal exotics, the biggest problems are rats, house mice, and cats. On some islands, the cats either escaped from fishermen or, in a few cases, were deliberately introduced to rid the island of rodents. Feral goats and burros live on Isla San José, and their voracious appetites are hard on the vegetation.

Bernie Tershy of Island Conservation, Alfonso Aguirre-Muñoz of Grupo Ecología y Conservación de Islas, and others are working to eradicate invasives. The Isla San Pedro Mártir rats were eradicated by 2007, and feral cats on Isla Santa Catalina seem to be gone.

Human impact on islands has included hunting and gathering of wild plant foods; cutting trees and shrubs for shelter, fuel, and baskets; setting fires; mining (for example, guano on Isla San Pedro Mártir, salt on Isla Carmen, and gypsum on Isla San Marcos); and introducing plants and animals, either deliberately or accidentally. Periodic setting of fires was done to encourage certain plants like chia (*Salvia columbariae*) that have edible seeds. Ironically, today, chia has become scarce on the mainland because of overgrazing and overharvesting.

Plus, these days the Baja Peninsula has been discovered by tourists, especially since Mexican Highway 1, traversing the peninsula's length, was paved, and modern, commercial airports were constructed in Loreto, La Paz, and San José del Cabo. Private interests are rapidly building resorts and golf courses along the Baja coast. The Mexican government has a development plan called Escalera Nautica ("nautical stairway"), which envisions twenty or more marinas from Bahía de Los Ángeles to Cabo San Lucas.

Some boaters in the Sea of Cortez do not take the remoteness of the place into consideration. One calm evening, our ship anchored off Isla Ángel de la Guarda, and we lowered the Zodiacs to take passengers on a circumnavigation of this awesome guano-encrusted rock. As I motored my Zodiac around the first corner, I saw two fellows waving frantically from a miniscule rock ledge barely above the sea. Their small boat was anchored just offshore.

I drove over to them to find out what they wanted. Turned out they were Americans who had come out to Ángel from the mainland to do a little fishing. However, their boat's engine had died, and they had been stranded here for days. We were the first people to come along.

They had plenty of fish and beer but no water to drink—very poor, and almost fatal, planning. Our ship's engineer took a look at their boat and determined that he didn't have the correct part to fix it. So our captain radioed mainland Mexico to have someone come out either with the part or to give these guys a tow to safety.

And it's not just tourists who get themselves into trouble in the Sea of Cortez. On Isla San Francisco, behind the beautiful, crescent-shaped, sandy beach, is a small salt pan, where Mexican fishermen occasionally come to collect salt for salting fish. On one of our visits, we came across a family—Mom and Dad and a couple of kids filling buckets. It was a hot sunny day, and these folks had been working hard for hours. Of course, the sudden intrusion of sixty curious American tourists was quite a spectacle and surprise to them. One of our naturalists went over to chat and discovered that this family did not have any drinking water.

FIGURE 50 This gypsum mine on Isla San Marcos is one of the few active mines in the gulf.

We radioed the ship and had several gallons brought over. The family, especially the kids, was very grateful. But we had to wonder why they hadn't bothered to bring water themselves.

Recently, I kayaked out to Isla Carmen. While sitting on the beach, sipping a cool Pacifico cerveza, a giant cruise ship steamed into view. This is a new phenomenon in the gulf. For several decades now, small cruise ships, private sailboats, and kayaks have been transporting visitors through the area and to the islands. However, the gargantuan cruise ships sailing along the Pacific coast would stop at Cabo San Lucas on Baja's southern tip briefly, but never venture into the gulf. Apparently this is changing.

As the sun dipped behind the distant peninsular mountains, a panga pulled in at the far end of the beach. Three Mexican fishermen climbed out and appeared to be settling in for the night. When it was almost dark, one of the fishermen came walking along the shore to our camp. He held up a lightbulb, an ordinary household, sixty-watt lightbulb, and seemed to be asking if we had some way to light it up. Now generally, I don't have a generator in my kayak or a very, very long extension cord, so I couldn't help him out. He shrugged, said "Gracias," and ambled back to his amigos. Maybe he thought that Americans have everything, including electricity in their kayaks.

All night long, whenever I briefly awoke and turned in my sleeping bag, I could hear the fishermen singing or talking. And before dawn, they were gone.

Throughout its history, Isla Carmen has been frequented by a different type of commercial ship—cargo ones. Massive salt deposits are found on the island. Lying just off the old Jesuit mother mission of Loreto, the salt has been mined more or less continuously since the seventeenth century. During the winter of 1841–1842, the ship *Naslednik Alexandr* arrived from Sitka, Alaska, to collect salt to preserve skins and fish. Aboard was I. G. Voznesenskii, a preparator for the Zoological Museum of the Russian Academy of Sciences in St. Petersburg. He made extensive botanical collections in the gulf area, probably becoming the first European to visit a gulf island and collect specimens. Unfortunately, his collection ended up in storage and was not re-discovered until nearly a century later.

During the 1850s, the demand for salt increased dramatically, and the Carmen salt works became the principal source for San Francisco. By 1867, 30,000 tons at $18 per ton were being shipped out, making the North American concessionaire, Ben Holladay, a very rich man. Since then, ownership has passed through a series of Mexican and foreign owners. Although salt mining has ceased, the island owners, Salinas del Pacifico, S.A., released desert bighorn sheep on Carmen in 1995. Conservationists are concerned about the sheep's impact.

In 1973, California Academy of Sciences biologist George Lindsay organized a trip to the Sea of Cortez with his friends—nature writer Joseph Wood Krutch, philanthropist Kenneth Bechtel, and national aviation hero turned conservationist Charles Lindbergh. They chartered a Catalina Flying Boat and flew to the gulf, exploring islands from Rocas Consag to Espíritu Santo.

The spectacular scenery and wildness thrilled them. A couple of months later, Lindsay and Lindbergh were in Mexico City to attend the premiere of a documentary about the Baja region sponsored by Bechtel. While there, Lindbergh requested an audience with Mexico's president Luis Echeverría. The president was abroad, but Lindbergh and Lindsay did meet with the president's cabinet, which, instead of hearing about

FIGURE 51   Old rusty tracks at the defunct salt mine on Isla Carmen.

some aspect of aviation, got an earful about the wonders of the gulf and its islands. Lindbergh spoke passionately about the wonders of the sea, especially the islands. Afterwards, he called the American ambassador to Mexico and asked to have a press conference arranged.

The Mexican media also expected an aviation talk, but Lindbergh expounded on the "wealth and beauty of the Sea of Cortez." Several years went by, but finally, in 1978, a decree was issued to protect all of the islands as wildlife refuges.

Over the last couple of decades, additional designations have been made to preserve the sea and its islands: Mexican President Carlos Salinas de Gortari decreed the Upper Gulf of California and Colorado River Delta Biosphere Reserve (1993); UNESCO's Man and the Biosphere Program dedicated the protected area of Islas del Golfo de California as an International Biosphere Reserve (1995); the Mexican federal government recategorized the islands as an Área de Protección de Flora y Fauna (2000); and UNESCO recognized the gulf and its islands as a World Heritage Site (2005).

The next morning, I pick up several discarded yellow plastic oil bottles and some other trash that has washed up on the beach on Carmen and stow it in my kayak. I slip into the cockpit and shove off into a crystalline, flat sea. I dip my paddle to begin the long journey back across to the peninsula. I hope my visit to this marvelous area has had only a minimal adverse impact.

Without warning, I am startled by several bottlenose dolphins as they break the surface and blow right next to me. I stop paddling, and they vanish. As I start again, they reappear. Obviously, they want to catch a bow wave for a free ride. I paddle as fast as I can and make only a pitiful ripple in the vast ocean. The dolphins realize that I am not much fun and veer off for something more exciting to do.

Even though my little paddle hardly makes a splash, if I put enough strokes together, eventually the kayak gets somewhere. Maybe, just maybe, we humans can be persistent enough and be diligent enough in our attempts to understand and protect this remarkable region to eventually make a difference. All the decrees and designations will not save the Sea of Cortez and its remarkable islands unless we who live, work, and play here make a commitment to take care of this special place. In the meantime, I'll keep paddling.

CIÉNEGA DE SANTA CLARA

Although not an island, one small biological bright spot in the upper gulf region is the forty-thousand-acre Ciénega de Santa Clara, a hypersaline lagoon near El Golfo de Santa Clara, the result of the Yuma Desalination Plant. By the 1960s, the area where the *ciénega* is today was a dry mudflat. Remarkably, however, the delivery of drainwater to this area resulted in the restoration of a highly productive wetland—even as the remainder of the delta ecosystem largely disappeared around it.

Today, the Ciénega de Santa Clara is home to thousands of migratory and resident birds and is a critical link in the Pacific Flyway. It harbors several endangered species, including at least 70 percent of the world's population of the endangered Yuma clapper rail. In recognition of the ciénega's central importance, Mexico has protected the wetlands by including it within the borders of the Upper Gulf of California and Colorado River Delta Biosphere Reserve. The ciénega is also internationally recognized as a wetland of great ecological significance. Desert pupfish (*Cyprinodon macularius*) live in the ciénega, which may be the last stronghold for this fascinating ice age relict species. As the largest remaining wetland in the Colorado River Delta, the ciénega functions as a critical component of the larger delta ecosystems.

Bibliography

Bowen, Thomas. 2000. *Unknown Island: Seri Indians, Europeans, and San Esteban Island in the Gulf of California.* University of New Mexico Press, Albuquerque.

Brusca, Richard C. 1980. *Common Intertidal Invertebrates of the Gulf of California.* University of Arizona Press, Tucson.

———. 2010. "Introduction." In *The Gulf of California: Biodiversity and Conservation,* edited by Richard C. Brusca. Arizona-Sonora Desert Museum Studies in Natural History. Arizona-Sonora Desert Museum Press; University of Arizona Press, Tucson.

Carabias-Lillo, J., J. de la Maza Elvira, D. Gutierrez-Carbonell, M. Gómez-Cruz, G. Anaya-Reyna, A. Zavala-Gonzáles, A. L. Figueroa and B. Bermúdez-Almada. 2000. *Programa de Manejo Área de Protección de Flora y Fauna Islas del Golfo de California.* Comisión Nacional de Áreas Naturales Protegidas, Mexico City.

Case, Ted J., and Martin L. Cody, eds. 1986. *Island Biogeography in the Sea of Cortéz.* University of California Press, Berkeley.

Case, Ted J., Martin L. Cody, and Exequiel Ezcurra, eds. 2002. *A New Island Biogeography in the Sea of Cortés.* Oxford University Press, New York.

Felger, Richard Stephen, and Bill Broyles, eds. 2007. *Dry Borders: Great Natural Reserves of the Sonoran Desert.* University of Utah Press, Salt Lake City.

Felger, Richard Stephen, and Mary Beck Moser. 1985. *People of the Desert and Sea: Ethnobotany of the Seri Indians.* University of Arizona Press, Tucson.

Gotshall, Daniel W. 1982. *Marine Animals of Baja California: A Guide to the Common Fish and Invertebrates.* Sea Challengers, Los Osos, California.

Grismer, L. Lee. 2002. *Amphibians and Reptiles of Baja California, Including Its Pacific Islands and the Islands in the Sea of Cortés.* University of California Press, Berkeley.

Hayden, Julian. 1998. *The Sierra Pinacate.* University of Arizona Press, Tucson.

Humphrey, Robert R. 1974. *The Boojum and Its Home.* University of Arizona Press, Tucson.

Hupp, Betty, and Marilyn Malone. 2008. *The Edge of the Sea of Cortez: Tidewalkers' Guide to the Upper Gulf of California.* Operculum, Tucson.

Johnson, William Weber. 1972. *Baja California.* Time-Life Books, New York.

Krutch, Joseph Wood. 1986. *The Forgotten Peninsula: A Naturalist in Baja California.* University of Arizona Press, Tucson.

Leopold, Aldo. 1968. *A Sand County Almanac: With Other Essays on Conservation from Round River.* 2nd ed. Oxford University Press, New York.

Lindblad, Sven-Olof, and Lisa Lindblad, eds. 1987. *Baja California.* Rizzoli, New York.

MacArthur, Robert H., and Edward O. Wilson. 1967. *The Theory of Island Biogeography.* Monographs in Population Biology, vol. 1. Princeton University Press, Princeton.

McGee, W. J., and Willard D. Johnson. 1896. "Seriland." *National Geographic Magazine* 7(4):125–133.

McPeak, Ron H. 2000. *Amphibians and Reptiles of Baja California.* Sea Challengers, Monterey, California.

Melville, Herman. 1851. *Moby-Dick; or, the Whale.* Harper & Bros., New York.

Minch, John, Edwin Minch, and Jason Minch. 1998. *Roadside Geology and Biology of Baja California.* John Minch and Associates, Mission Viejo, California.

Nabhan, Gary Paul. 1985. *Gathering the Desert.* University of Arizona Press, Tucson.

Olin, George. 1994. *House in the Sun: A Natural History of the Sonoran Desert.* Southwest Parks and Monuments Association, Tucson.

Quammen, David. 1996. *The Song of the Dodo: Island Biogeography in an Age of Extinction.* Scribner, New York.

Roberts, Norman C. 1989. *Baja California Plant Field Guide*. Natural History Pub. Co., La Jolla, California.

Romano-Lax, Andromeda. 1993. *Sea Kayaking in Baja*. Wilderness Press, Berkeley, California.

———. 2002. *Searching for Steinbeck's Sea of Cortez: A Makeshift Expedition along Baja's Desert Coast*. Sasquatch Books, Seattle, Washington.

Schoenherr, Allan A. 1992. *A Natural History of California*. University of California Press, Berkeley.

Schoenherr, Allan A., C. Robert Feldmeth, and Michael J. Emerson. 1999. *Natural History of the Islands of California*. University of California Press, Berkeley.

Sowell, John. 2001. *Desert Ecology*. University of Utah Press, Salt Lake City.

Steinbeck, John. 1941. *The Log from the Sea of Cortez*. Viking Press, New York.

Terrill, Ceiridwen. 2007. *Unnatural Landscapes: Tracking Invasive Species*. University of Arizona Press, Tucson.

Walker, Lewis W. 1951. "Sea Birds of Isla Raza [sic], Baja California." *National Geographic Magazine*, 99(2):239–248.

Wauer, Roland H. 1992. *Naturalist's Mexico*. Texas A&M University Press, College Station.

Wiggins, Ira L. 1980. *Flora of Baja California*. Stanford University Press, Palo Alto, California.

Winchester, Simon. 2003. *Krakatoa: The Day the World Exploded: August 27, 1883*. Harper Collins, New York.

Zwinger, Ann. 1983. *A Desert Country near the Sea: A Natural History of the Cape Region of Baja California*. Harper & Row, New York.

About the Author

Stewart Aitchison is a zoologist and geologist by training and a naturalist and photographer by passion. He has been exploring, photographing, teaching, and writing about the Colorado Plateau for more than forty years, ten of those as a field biologist for the Museum of Northern Arizona in Flagstaff. Besides leading trips for Lindblad Expeditions, he also escorts educational excursions for the National Audubon Society, Smithsonian Institution, Grand Canyon Field Institute, National Geographic Expeditions, Elderhostel, and other educational groups across the globe. Some of his latest publications include *Grand Canyon's North Rim and Beyond; Grand Canyon: Window of Time; A Traveler's Guide to Monument Valley*; and *A Guide to Southern Utah's Hole-in-the-Rock Trail*. A complete list of his books can be found at www.stewartaitchison.com. When not out in the field, Stewart and his wife Ann split their time between Flagstaff, Arizona, and Bluff, Utah.